Bullsh*t

500 MIND-BLOWING LIES
WE STILL BELIEVE

KATIE ADAMS

CASTLE POINT BOOKS

NEW YORK

www.castlepointbooks.com

The Castle Point Books trademark is owned by
Castle Point Publishing, LLC. Castle Point books are
published and distributed by St. Martin's Press.

ISBN 978-1-250-27007-8 (trade paperback)
ISBN 978-1-250-25353-8 (ebook)

Cover design by Katie Jennings Campbell
Interior design by Melissa Gerber
Interior composition by Noora Cox

Images used under license by Shutterstock.com

Our books may be purchased in bulk for promotional, educational,
or business use. Please contact your local bookseller or the
Macmillan Corporate and Premium Sales Department at
1-800-221-7945, extension 5442, or by email at
MacmillanSpecialMarkets@macmillan.com.

First Edition: April 2020

10 9 8 7 6 5 4 3 2 1

CONTENTS

"Believe nothing
you hear, and only
one half that you see."

—Edgar Allan Poe, "The System of
Dr. Tarr and Professor Fether"

Wait a Minute...This is Bullsh*t!

As human beings, we all seem to share a natural desire to know "the truth." To understand the world around us makes it less frightening, and it's easier to live our lives if we think we have some semblance of control, which comes from acquiring knowledge. However, as centuries of oral traditions, fairy tales, books, and movies show, we all also love a good story.

And therein lies the problem. An interesting, well-told, dramatic tale is sometimes (if not often) more exciting—and memorable—than the truth. This is how rumors, myths, tall tales, legends, lies, and misconceptions get started... and spread. There's also the matter of learning the facts about life from those we love or trust—parents, teachers, leaders—then they simply *have* to be true. Never mind that your mother and your fifth-grade teacher didn't exactly check their sources when they told you that "you lose 90 percent of your body heat through your head" or that "Columbus proved the world was round."

Bearing that in mind, it's a great big world with a lot of great big lies. Here are 500 bits of well-known knowledge and conventional wisdom that are, well, *Bullsh*t*. Ready to find out... *the truth?*

Chapter 1

America the Mythical

There's a bit more to those stories about the Founding Fathers, the Pilgrims, and the American way of life that you've heard a million times. For example: the truth.

SALEM'S LOT

Bullsh*t!

Those found guilty in the Salem Witch Trials were burned at the stake.

Truth:

In the Salem Witch Trials of the 1690s, 20 people (mostly women) were found guilty and executed, and they were hanged, all except for Giles Corey, who was crushed to death under the weight of stones.

THE PLANE TRUTH

Bullsh*t!

Charles Lindbergh became an American hero and celebrity after he piloted the *Spirit of St. Louis* over the Atlantic Ocean, the first person to do so.

Truth:

Lindbergh was the 61st person to fly over the Atlantic...but the first person to do it solo.

SCHOOL'S OUT

Bullsh*t!

American schools' summer vacation originated with farm families' pulling their kids out of school to help with chores.

Truth:

In the 19th century, before the days of air conditioning, schoolhouses got so hot in the summer months that wealthy parents took their kids out of school in June, July, and August and would retreat to their country houses. Then the middle classes started doing it, and before long, so few kids were showing up for summer school that administrators canceled classes.

A CHERRY BAD DAY

Bullsh*t!

President Zachary Taylor died in 1850 after eating a ton of cherries and washing them down with milk, a toxic combination when mixed.

Truth:

While Taylor did dine on fruit and cow juice on the Fourth of July, five days before his death, it was cholera that killed him.

ROUND 'EM UP

Bullsh*t!

During times of attack by Native Americans, Old West pioneers would circle their wagons.

Truth:

That just looked dramatic in old cowboy movies. When settlers really did circle their wagons on the frontier, it was to "fence in" livestock.

THE MILD WEST

Bullsh*t!

The Old West was the Wild West, full of shootouts, murder, and pioneer justice.

Truth:

During what historians consider the golden age of the Old West, 1870 to 1885, the major settlements of Dodge City, Ellsworth, Abilene, Caldwell, and Wichita experienced 45 murders, combined. The murder rate in the 21st-century U.S. is about five times that.

NOT THE PEROT YOU KNOW

Bullsh*t!

President George Bush would've won re-election in 1992 if not for the candidacy of H. Ross Perot.

Truth:

The 1992 presidential election was the first in decades to feature three major candidates: Democrat Bill Clinton, Republican Bush, and Perot, a billionaire from Texas running as an independent. Perot held himself up as a populist, a financial conservative and political outsider, and he won 19 percent of the popular vote. As he leaned to the right of the political spectrum, conventional wisdom held that without Perot in the race, Bush would've gotten that 19 percent, enough to triumph over Clinton. Post-election exit polls indicated that Perot siphoned off votes equally from Clinton and Bush.

YOU'RE FREE (NOT SO FAST)

Bullsh*t!

Slavery officially ended when President Abraham Lincoln issued the Emancipation Proclamation in 1862.

Truth:

Most northern states had long outlawed slavery; therefore, the Emancipation Proclamation was an expression of U.S. government authority over the rogue Southern states that had seceded, so they didn't much pay attention to Lincoln's order. Five states remained loyal to the Union during the Civil War but still used slavery—Kentucky, Missouri, West Virginia, Maryland, and Delaware—and the Emancipation Proclamation allowed that practice to continue there. Slavery was eliminated nationwide with the passage of the Thirteenth Amendment in 1865.

THIS STORY IS FULL OF GORE

Bullsh*t!

Al Gore claimed to have invented the Internet.

Truth:

In a presidential campaign interview with CNN in 1999, Gore said, "During my service in the United States Congress, I took the initiative in creating the Internet. I took the initiative in moving forward a whole range of initiatives that have proven to be important to our country's economic growth and environmental protection, improvements in our educational system."

THE NAME GAME

Bullsh*t!

When millions of people immigrated to the United States through Ellis Island, officials changed their names to make them easier to pronounce or to sound more "American."

Truth:

Records of immigrants were generated from ship manifests, so there was no chance or reason to rename anyone. If immigrants' names changed, the immigrants made the change themselves, informing processors of their new name when they were getting checked off the manifest.

CAMP OUT

Bullsh*t!

The only group the U.S. government placed in internment camps during World War II were Japanese people.

Truth:

About 11,500 people of German descent were interned during World War II

ES IST NICHT WAHR

Bullsh*t!

Americans would speak German today if a Congressional vote to make it the official language of the U.S. had passed.

Truth:

Not quite. By the 1770s, when talk of Revolution hung in the air, some representatives to the Continental Congress so thoroughly hated their English overlords that they bandied about the symbolic idea to make something other than English an official language of the new nation. While Hebrew, Greek, and Spanish were discussed, German garnered the most support. A congressional vote to make German the official language failed, 28 to 27. (But had it passed, that wouldn't mean everyone would've suddenly started speaking German; Canada is officially bilingual, but only about 20 percent of its citizens speak both English and French.)

RON ANSWER

Bullsh*t!

President Ronald Reagan suffered from Alzheimer's during his administration.

Truth:

He was diagnosed with the condition in 1994, five years after leaving office.

BOOK IT

Bullsh*t!

Elected officials must swear to uphold their oath of service on a Bible.

Truth:

They can use any book they want.

DON'T HAVE A COW

Bullsh*t!

The Great Chicago Fire of 1871 began when "Mrs. O'Leary's cow" knocked over a lantern during a milking session.

Truth:

The devastating fire did begin in the O'Leary family's (unoccupied) barn, and high winds and dry air quickly spread it. Investigators never did find the cause, speculating in the report that it could have been "a spark blown from a chimney." After the fire was extinguished, *Chicago Republican* reporter Michael Ahern wrote up the story about O'Leary's cow and a fateful kick to a lantern. Such a vivid, visceral story easily spread, and nobody much noticed in 1893 when Ahern admitted he made up the whole thing.

THEY GAVE PEACE A CHANCE

Bullsh*t!

Soldiers returning home from fighting in the Vietnam War were spit on by anti-war protestors.

Truth:

There's no record of this happening. It's a rumor started by pro-military forces to discredit the anti-war movement.

CHEW ON THIS

Bullsh*t!

George Washington had wooden teeth.

Truth:

He wore several pairs of crude dentures constructed out of various materials, including ivory, gold, lead...and other people's teeth.

POWDER POWER

Bullsh*t!

All colonial men wore powdered wigs.

Truth:

While wigs were in fashion, they were also (like a lot of fashionable things) very expensive. Lawyers, politicians, and other men with lucrative cushy jobs could afford to wear them, and they did. They wouldn't be a very practical choice for blue-collar workers (who wouldn't have earned enough money to buy one anyway).

IF THE NAME FITS

Bullsh*t!

The U.S. president has always lived in the White House.

Truth:

The first Commander-in-Chief to live and work at 1600 Pennsylvania Avenue was John Adams, the second president. And it wasn't even called the White House until 1901, earning that name during the administration of Theodore Roosevelt. Prior to that, it was called, variously, the Executive Mansion, the President's House, and the President's Palace.

A COLONIAL BAKER'S DOZEN

Bullsh*t!

The American Revolution began when 13 English colonies revolted.

Truth:

The uprising was the concerted effort of 12 colonies—Delaware was a part of Pennsylvania until June 1776.

Bullsh*t!

In 1867, Secretary of State William Seward bought the Alaska Territory from Russia. This acquisition of supposedly useless land was unpopular and came to be known as "Seward's Folly."

Truth:

Dozens of newspapers of the time published editorials in favor of the purchase, citing positives like increased trade with Asia, building diplomatic relations with Russia, and increasing the size of the United States. The widely read *New York Tribune*, published by Seward's political rival Horace Greeley, came out against the purchase.

AND THE WAR DRAGGED ON

Bullsh*t!

The Civil War ended in April 1865, when Robert E. Lee surrendered to Ulysses S. Grant at Appomattox Courthouse in Virginia.

Truth:

That surrender covered only Lee's Army of Northern Virginia, the Confederacy's largest force. Several other battalions continued to fight, giving up the ghost weeks and even months later.

FLYING LOW

Bullsh*t!

If a U.S. flag touches the ground, by law it must be burned.

Truth:

Federal law requires a flag to be destroyed, "preferably by burning," only when it gets old, ratty, and "no longer a fitting emblem for display."

Bullsh*t!

The people who left England on the *Mayflower* and settled in Plymouth, Massachusetts, were called the Pilgrims.

Truth:

They were known as Old Comers. In 1820, statesman and orator Daniel Webster spoke at an event commemorating the 200th anniversary of the founding of Plymouth, and he called them "pilgrim fathers," and that name caught on.

PHONING IT IN

Bullsh*t!

A "red phone" in the Oval Office provided a direct line to the Kremlin in the Soviet Union.

Truth:

Set up in 1963, the direct line between the U.S. and U.S.S.R. wasn't red, and it wasn't a phone. It was a telegraph connection that could take as long as 12 hours to send and receive messages.

HATS ON!

Bullsh*t!

Cowboys wore cowboy hats—the Stetson style.

Truth:

The Stetson wasn't available for commercial purchase until 1865, and it didn't sell well until about 1895. Up to that time, Old West guys wore all kinds of hats, usually flat caps, derby hats, and sombreros.

NOT A BLACK-AND-WHITE STORY

Bullsh*t!

The Pilgrims dressed in black and wore hats with buckles on them.

Truth:

We don't really know how the Pilgrims dressed in the 1600s, because there's no visual or written record. In the early 1800s, artists started to produce paintings of the Pilgrims. Since they didn't know what they wore, they just depicted them wearing the clothing styles of the early 1800s.

JUST PLANE FALSE

Bullsh*t!

Air Force One is an airplane.

Truth:

While the president usually makes use of a specific aircraft, *Air Force One* is the designation given to any plane on which the president is currently traveling.

RING, RING

Bullsh*t!

Philadelphia's Liberty Bell rang—and then cracked right down the middle— on the important day of July 4, 1776.

Truth:

The landmark was called the State House Bell until slavery abolitionists in the mid-1800s convinced the nation to call it the Liberty Bell. And no celebrating revolutionaries rang and cracked it on the first Independence Day, because it had started to split in 1752.

AN EARLY CUT

As a boy, George Washington cut down a beloved cherry tree and owned up to it because he "couldn't tell a lie."

Truth:

The story goes that six-year-old Washington was given a hatchet, and in playing with it, cut down his father's cherry tree. When confronted, young Washington said, "I cannot tell a lie, I did cut it with my hatchet." His father was proud of his honest son. The story was proof that America's father was a kind and just man, and it originated in the 1806 edition of *The Life of Washington* by Mason Locke Weems, who completely made up the story.

FLIGHT TEST

Bullsh*t!

The president and the vice-president of the United States are not legally allowed to fly on the same plane...in case of a deadly crash.

Truth:

It's an unofficial suggestion, not a rule or a law, and many presidents and their number-twos have flown in *Air Force One* together.

REBEL, REBEL

Bullsh*t!

The flag of the Confederacy is the "rebel flag"—a blue X against a red background.

Truth:

This was never an official symbol or flag of the Confederate States of America, which used three different banners during the Civil War.

CONTROLLED BURN

Bullsh*t!

Feminist protests in the 1960s included a symbolic gesture of their rejection of the patriarchy: burning bras.

Truth:

A small group of feminists protested the 1968 Miss America Pageant in Atlantic City, New Jersey. Protestors planned to burn their bras—paralleling the burning of Vietnam War-era draft cards—but police stopped them from doing so. That fact, and how they threw their bras in trash cans, became conflated in the public consciousness.

A CODED MESSAGE

Bullsh*t!

Samuel Morse invented Morse Code.

Truth:

Morse is credited with the invention of the telegraph, but Morse Code, the language used to send messages via telegraph, was largely the work of his assistant, Alfred Vail.

CAR TROUBLE

Bullsh*t!

Henry Ford invented the automobile (and the assembly line).

Truth:

Karl Benz (as in Mercedes-Benz) built the first working, modern automobile in 1885, while Ransom Olds (as in Oldsmobile) came up with the assembly line.

ALL FOR ONE

Bullsh*t!

A jury must always return a unanimous verdict.

Truth:

In U.S. federal courts, and in criminal trials at the state level (in almost every state), a full consensus is required. About a third of the states don't require a unanimous verdict for civil trials—a simple majority will suffice.

THIS ONE IS SHOCKING

Bullsh*t!

Benjamin Franklin discovered electricity with his famous kite-and-key-and-lightning experiment.

Truth:

Franklin didn't conduct the experiment—he wrote about it as a *possible* experiment.

FOR THE BIRDS

Bullsh*t!

Benjamin Franklin argued that the turkey should be the United States' national symbol.

Truth:

In a letter to his daughter, Franklin expressed his displeasure over the selection of the eagle, which he found to be "a bird of bad moral character. He does not get his living honestly." He also didn't think the illustration of the eagle on the National Seal was all that great, saying that it "looks more like a turkey," which was fine with him because "the turkey is in comparison a much more respectable bird, and withal a true original native of America."

HATS OFF!

Bullsh*t!

American men wore hats until 1961, when John F. Kennedy appeared hatless at his presidential inauguration, inspiring everybody to take their hats off, too.

Truth:

Fashions come and fashions go, and in that regard, the men's hat slowly fell out of favor throughout the '60s. And Kennedy wore a hat for much of Inauguration Day.

MR. KING PRESIDENT

Bullsh*t!

The news media coined the term "Camelot" to describe the youthful, idealistic administration of John F. Kennedy, harkening back to the romanticized King Arthur legends.

Truth:

It first appeared in a *Life* article about Kennedy published after his assassination. His widow, former First Lady Jacqueline Kennedy, made the comparison.

IT'S NO SECRET

Bullsh*t!

The Secret Service's sole job is to protect the President and the First Family.

Truth:

Only a small division of the agency is responsible for keeping the President safe. The organization's primary aim, and the reason it was created in 1865, is to fight counterfeiting.

THE COST OF MANHATTAN

Bullsh*t!

European settlers purchased the island of Manhattan for $24.

Truth:

In 1626, the Lenape tribe did sell Manhattan to the leaders of New Netherland. The agreed-upon sum: 60 guilders. When 19th-century historians repeated this fact, they calculated 60 guilders to equal $24. But in 21st-century money, it's more like $1,000. That's still a low price for a couple of huge islands, but the Lenape weren't dumb. Historians say they didn't believe people really "owned" land, and that in all likelihood they considered the transaction with New Netherland to be more of a long-term rental than a purchase.

CAROLINA GOLD

Bullsh*t!

America's first "gold rush" began in California in 1849.

Truth:

In 1799, a 12-year-old uncovered a 17-pound golf nugget in Cabarrus County, North Carolina. Before long, more than 30,000 gold prospectors had settled in the area.

WATCH WHAT YOU SAY

Bullsh*t!

The First Amendment guarantees Americans "freedom of speech," or the right to say anything they want.

Truth:

Truth: The First Amendment merely prevents the government from placing any restrictions on speech or other forms of communication.

Lincoln and Kennedy

Are there tons of eerie coincidences between the lives of Abraham Lincoln and John F. Kennedy? This idea has been the premise of countless articles and email forward lists, and it first circulated in 1964, less than a year after Kennedy's death. Many items on the list are true but mundane—"Lincoln" and "Kennedy" both have seven letters—while others are totally false. While Kennedy had "a secretary named Lincoln," Lincoln did not have a "secretary named Kennedy." The claim that both presidential assassins, John Wilkes Booth and Lee Harvey Oswald, were known by three names isn't true, as Kennedy's assailant went by Lee Oswald. The list also asserts that Booth "ran from a theater and was caught in a warehouse," while Oswald "ran from a warehouse and was caught in a theater." Booth was caught in a barn on a tobacco farm.

ONE GIANT
SHRUG FOR MANKIND

Bullsh*t!

Americans were thrilled to put a man on the moon.

Truth:

In the years between 1961, when President John F. Kennedy asked NASA to
send astronauts to the moon, and 1969, when NASA actually did it, public
support topped 50 percent only in the days before *Apollo 11* landed on the
lunar surface. Throughout the decade, the space program routinely ranked
at the top of federal programs that polled Americans thought should be cut
to save money.

ONLY THE MARKET PLUNGED

Bullsh*t!

In the wake of the stock market crash of 1929, dozens of distraught
investors who suddenly lost everything jumped off New York's many
skyscrapers to their deaths.

Truth:

There's no record of a single crash-related jumping death. However, Winston
Churchill was staying in New York on that day in October 1929, and he
reported seeing a man sail past his hotel room window. That man was a
German chemist who accidentally fell out of a 16th floor window. That
death was reported along with the Wall Street hysteria, forever linking
the two events.

Chapter 2

The Human Body

There are so many things that your doctor and your high school biology teacher just got completely wrong about how you and all your parts work.

HOT HEAD

Bullsh*t!

You lose most of your body heat through the top of your head.

Truth:

Bundle up your whole body, and wear a hat, in the winter—you lose body heat equally from all over.

COLD FRONT

Bullsh*t!

The common cold is a single, specific viral infection.

Truth:

Each year, different strains of "the cold" attack, and everyone who gets it builds up an immunity. Then that virus mutates to the point where nobody's immune system recognizes it anymore and it gets everybody sick again. And even then, it's not one specific virus—in any given year about 100 viruses of this nature circulate.

C WHAT HAPPENS

Bullsh*t!

Large doses of vitamin C can prevent a cold.

Truth:

It may slightly reduce the severity of a cold after you've acquired one. Also, any vitamin C you've consumed beyond what your body absolutely needs leaves the body via urine.

Bullsh*t!

Cold medicine cuts down the duration of a cold.

Truth:

Cold pills help dampen the symptoms of the cold for four to six hours or so. The only real "cure" for the cold is time—the body processes the sickness over seven to ten days.

THE BIG COVER-UP

Bullsh*t!

You can catch a cold, the flu, or even pneumonia by going out in cold weather not properly dressed or with wet hair.

Truth:

Colds, the flu, and pneumonia are caused by germs...not cold air.

WORTH A SHOT

Bullsh*t!

A flu shot can make you sick.

Truth:

Some flu vaccines can make you feel a little "off" after you get them...for a day or so. If you get sick after a flu shot, the flu shot didn't make you sick—a strain of flu or cold not covered by that vaccine already in your body did.

THE FLU IN YOU

Bullsh*t!

Stomach flu can get you very sick.

Truth:

Flu, short for influenza, is a viral respiratory illness. A "stomach flu" isn't a type of influenza—it's gastroenteritis.

URINE TROUBLE

Bullsh*t!

Peeing on a jellyfish sting immediately after the attack will soothe the pain and help it heal faster.

Truth:

Throwing some seawater on a sting works best, along with vinegar. So clearly, somewhere along the line, somebody thought that urine—which is both salty and vinegary—was the best medicine.

WE ARE THE 10 PERCENT!

Bullsh*t!

Humans use only about 10 percent of our brains.

Truth:

That's something motivational speakers and teachers say to get people to use their full potential. From a biological standpoint, almost every part of the brain controls some bodily function or purpose. Humans use about *100* percent of their noggins.

MAKES A LOT OF SENSE

Bullsh*t!
Humans have five senses.

Truth:
Depending on which branch of science you consult, humans have somewhere between nine and 21 senses. We're capable of interpreting clues and data from the world around us beyond just sight, sound, smell, taste, and touch. For example, we can sense temperature, pain, and balance.

WATER HAZARD

Bullsh*t!
If you go swimming immediately after eating, you'll get a stomach cramp, and that could make you drown.

Truth:
If you swim less than 30 minutes after a meal, you *might* get a minor arm cramp for a second (the blood that would be there is serving the stomach), but not a deadly stomach cramp.

TUMMY TROUBLE

Bullsh*t!
When you're hungry, your stomach rumbles.

Truth:
The stomach sits higher in your body than you think—it's behind the lower ribs. Your "belly" is actually the small intestine...which is what rumbles when you need a snack.

NAILED IT

Bullsh*t!

Hair and fingernails continue to grow after death.

Truth:

Shortly after the body dies, it starts to lose moisture and dries out. The skin around the nails and hairlines shrinks and recedes as a result, giving the impression that things are longer—but they're just more exposed.

HOW SWEET IT IS

Bullsh*t!

Sugar makes kids hyperactive.

Truth:

One study came out in the mid-1970s that linked sugar consumption to kids' acting wild—the gist of which was that a doctor took the sugar out of one kid's diet and the child sat still more. But more than a dozen studies have shown quite the opposite, that sugar doesn't lead to hyperactivity. So, then, if it's not the cake, why are kids so charged up during a birthday party? Because it's a *party*—they're overstimulated.

NO KIDNEY-ING!

Bullsh*t!

When you've got a bad kidney, you can get a kidney transplant to replace it.

Truth:

Doctors don't remove the old kidney, as doing so is tricky, dangerous, and can increase patient mortality. Instead, the new kidney is just added into the body.

WAKEY-WAKEY

Bullsh*t!

It's neurologically dangerous to wake a sleepwalker.

Truth:

You should absolutely wake up a sleepwalker, especially if they're about to wander into traffic or something. This idea comes from an old superstition that states a sleepwalker's spirit leaves their body during their nocturnal adventures, and, if the walker is awakened, that spirit may not come back.

SCHOOL OF HARD KNOCKS

Bullsh*t!

It's unsafe to let a person believed to have suffered a concussion fall asleep.

Truth:

If, after suffering the injury, the individual is alert and able to carry on a conversation, and their symptoms aren't getting worse, they can go ahead and get some shut-eye.

SHAVE IT FOR LATER

Bullsh*t!

Any hair you shave will grow back thicker...and darker.

Truth:

How hair grows is determined almost entirely by your individual genetic makeup. Shaving affects it not at all.

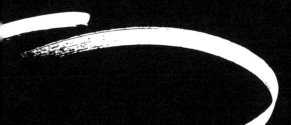

LET'S SPLIT

Bullsh*t!

Some hair products can repair split ends and hair that's otherwise damaged.

Truth:

They just smooth it down and mask the problem...that's why you must keep using them day after day.

THIRSTY?

Bullsh*t!

People need to drink eight glasses of water a day or they'll get dehydrated.

Truth:

Everybody needs a different amount of water, depending on their weight, activity level, and environmental factors. Also, liquid consumed via fruits, vegetables, juices, tea, and the like helps keep the body hydrated.

FEEL THE BURN

Bullsh*t!

If you stop exercising regularly, your muscle will turn to fat.

Truth:

Muscle and fat are completely different body tissues with different compositions, and so one can't transform into the other. If you used to be ripped and are now chubby, it's because you're exercising less and/or eating more.

SEEMS LIKE A STRETCH

Bullsh*t!
Stretch before you exercise so your muscles don't get sore later.

Truth:
Stretching warms up the muscles and helps to prevent injury, but it won't prevent soreness.

STEP OFF

Bullsh*t!
You need to take 10,000 steps each day to stay in shape.

Truth:
There's no known benefit or science to this number. It comes from a Japanese pedometer manufacturer, because the Japanese character for 10,000 steps looks like a person walking.

BIG NEWS

Bullsh*t!
Some people look overweight, or "fat," but they're actually just "big-boned."

Truth:
People carry their weight in soft tissue—muscle and fat. Extra-large or extra-thick bones aren't really a thing. The term "big-boned" is used to make heavy people not feel bad about being heavy.

AW, SHIRT!

Bullsh*t!
Sweat causes "pit stains."

Truth:
The active ingredient in many deodorants is aluminum, and when that chemically reacts to the protein in sweat, it turns yellow.

NOW HEAR THIS

Bullsh*t!
Your ears are those floppy things on the sides of your head.

Truth:
The ear is a complex system with many parts. The external parts are called *pinnae*, and they're mostly made of cartilage. They funnel and direct sound into the head...which is where the hard-working inner ear and middle ear process sound.

SPEAK UP, SONNY

Bullsh*t!
Your hearing gets worse the older you get—it's a symptom of aging.

Truth:
Most people's hearing does worsen as they age, but it's not because of the natural degradation of the body. Years of accumulated exposure to noise weakens your ears over time.

READING TIP

Bullsh*t!
Reading in dim light hurts your eyes.

Truth:
While it can certainly be difficult and straining to read a book you can barely see, the American Academy of Ophthalmology says that the practice "causes no permanent eye damage."

A DARK VIEW

Bullsh*t!
Watching TV in a dark room is bad for your eyes.

Truth:
Sure, if you believe J. Robert Mendte, an ad man who in the 1950s spread this notion in commercials for a lamp company.

WISE CRACK

Bullsh*t!
Cracking your knuckles makes them bigger and causes arthritis.

Truth:
It's a habit that grosses out and annoys some people...who likely spread this myth.

STEP OFF

Bullsh*t!

Stepping on a rusty nail can give you a tetanus infection.

Truth:

The bacterium that causes the infection is found in generally unclean areas where the same things that cause metal to rust can be found, like dusty old barns. If you get a tetanus infection after visiting such a place, it's not because you also stepped on a nail.

GOT MILK?

Bullsh*t!

White spots on the fingernails indicate a calcium deficiency.

Truth:

Nope. Just evidence of a minor injury, like getting your finger caught in a drawer.

PINS AND NEEDLES

Bullsh*t!

An arm or a leg "falls asleep" because you've somehow cut off the blood supply, by sitting weirdly or something like that.

Truth:

A sleeping appendage, or *paresthesia*, is the result of the pathway between nerves in that limb and the brain getting cut off or blocked due to sustained pressure.

NOT SO FUNNY

Bullsh*t!

Bang your elbow and feel a weird jolt? You hit your funny bone!

Truth:

The body doesn't respond like that when bones get hit. They do when *nerves* get struck unpleasantly, however. The "funny bone" is really the ulnar nerve.

TOXIC RELATIONSHIP

Bullsh*t!

"Cleanse" products remove toxins, which can build up and cause poor health.

Truth:

They're useless. It's the job of the kidneys and liver to remove toxins. If they don't do that, and they're not functioning properly, you die.

GREASE IS THE WORD

Bullsh*t!

Poor diet causes acne.

Truth:

Hey, teens—the fat in French fries and chocolate doesn't magically travel up to your face and make it greasy and zit-covered. How much or how little acne you get is determined by genetic factors.

BLUE BLOOD

Bullsh*t!
Deoxygenated blood is blue.

Truth:
It's deep red.

IRONING OUT THE WRINKLES

Bullsh*t!
Submersion in water makes the skin absorb that water and then wrinkle and swell.

Truth:
The autonomic nervous system triggers a constriction of the blood vessels, causing a wrinkled look.

HEY BUD

Bullsh*t!
Different "zones" on the tongue sense the different kinds of tastes—sweet, salty, bitter, etc.

Truth:
Taste buds all over the tongue taste every different taste, while some areas may be ever so slightly more sensitive to the different kinds.

CHEW ON THIS

Bullsh*t!

Don't swallow that gum—it'll take your body seven whole years to digest.

Truth:

Apart from the sugar and flavoring, chewing gum is indigestible, which means that your body will simply, um, pass it in a timely fashion.

HEY BRAINIAC

Bullsh*t!

The two hemispheres of the brain—the left and right—are responsible for different skills.

Truth:

There's no real division between the two sides. The left brain can learn "right brain" tasks, and vice versa.

HAVE A SEAT

Bullsh*t!

You can catch a disease from a toilet seat.

Truth:

Doctors have never linked the transmission of any disease to toilet seats, which are generally too cold and not porous enough to provide a proper home for insidious germs.

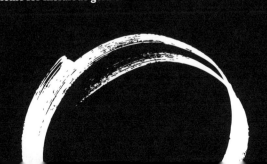

ROLL IT UP

Bullsh*t!

The ability to roll your tongue is genetic.

Truth:

Tongue rolling is often given as an example of a hereditary trait in basic science classes, but it's just not true. You can roll your tongue, or you can learn to roll your tongue...or you can't. It has nothing to do with your bloodline.

GET BENT

Bullsh*t!

Some people are double-jointed.

Truth:

Nope, they're just extremely flexible or have an above-average range of motion.

THAT BIOLOGICAL CLOCK

Bullsh*t!

It's hard for a woman to get pregnant after age 35 because that's when her fertility drops by as much as 50 percent.

Truth:

Women trying to have a baby at age 27 have an 86 percent success rate, and women at age 37 have an 82 percent success rate.

KISSIN' COUSINS

Bullsh*t!

Children who result from first cousins breeding are more likely to experience deformities.

Truth:

Chances of birth defects in cousin-love are a hair higher than in babies born to non-related parents. It's something that's said to discourage interfamilial relationships, a social taboo.

CLEAR!

Bullsh*t!

A defibrillator restarts the heart by delivering a powerful electronic shock that quickly brings the patient back to life and consciousness.

Truth:

A defibrillator re-synchronizes all chambers of the heart to get it beating again, and that's just the first of several steps in saving a patient's life.

GOOD PROGNOSIS

Bullsh*t!

Melanoma and skin cancer are the same thing.

Truth:

Melanoma is a type of skin cancer. It accounts for only 1 percent of all skin cancer diagnoses, but is responsible for almost all skin cancer-related deaths.

THIS IS DEPRESSING

Bullsh*t!

Clinical depression is caused by a chemical imbalance in the brain.

Truth:

Scientists have yet to discover a physical cause for depression. The idea that it's a chemical problem comes from pharmaceutical companies selling treatment options.

WRONG CONDITION

Bullsh*t!

People with schizophrenia experience multiple personalities.

Truth:

That's multiple personality disorder, or dissociative identity disorder. A suite of symptoms characterizes schizophrenia, most of them having to do with a confusion between what is and isn't reality.

IT'S COMPLICATED

Bullsh*t!

Dyslexia is characterized by words or letters appearing backward.

Truth:

It's way more nuanced than that. People with dyslexia are otherwise of normal intelligence but have difficulties mentally processing written language, such as in spelling and reading comprehension.

TAKE A PICTURE

Bullsh*t!

A handful of individuals have "photographic memory," or the ability to remember images or events with extreme accuracy.

Truth:

No one has ever been proven to have this gift. Candidates tested generally had good memory-building skills and abilities to begin with, coupled with the use techniques to do even better, particularly mnemonic devices.

GOTTA GO

Bullsh*t!

During a night of drinking, "breaking the seal" and going to the bathroom for the first time means you'll be going to the bathroom every five minutes until last call.

Truth:

There's no science there. The reason you have to keep peeing is because you're drinking a lot of liquid.

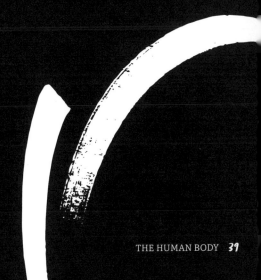

JAVA JOLT

Bullsh*t!

Coffee can help a drunk person sober up quickly.

Truth:

The caffeine in coffee does to a drunk person what it does to a sober person: increases alertness. Coffee doesn't change blood alcohol level at all.

BAD DOG

Bullsh*t!

Some "hair of the dog that bit you"—a little bit of alcohol, in other words—cures a hangover.

Truth:

A hangover—with its headache, nausea, and other symptoms—begins when the body's blood alcohol level hits 0. Having a drink brings that level back up, but only for a little while. It only serves to delay hangover symptoms.

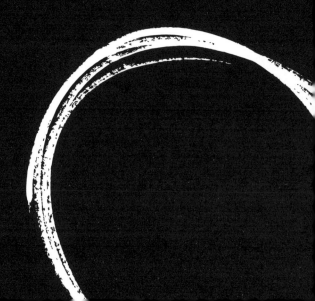

Chapter 3

It's Only Natural

Yes, it's only natural indeed to want to learn how animals and plants really behave.

ALL PACKED UP

Bullsh*t!
Camels store water in their humps.

Truth:
Camel humps are filled with fat.

GOOD DAY, MATE

Bullsh*t!
Penguins mate for life.

Truth:
Emperor penguins are serially monogamous, meaning they mate with only one partner during one breeding season, then mate with a different penguin the next year.

OLÉ!

Bullsh*t!
Bulls get angry when they see red.

Truth:
Bulls are colorblind. What agitates them isn't the color of the bullfighter's flag, but the motion, which they perceive as a threat.

KEEP YOUR HEAD DOWN

Bullsh*t!
When threatened by predators, ostriches bury their heads in the sand, thinking that they can't be seen.

Truth:
These birds have small heads, and when they peck at the ground for food, it may look like they're burying their heads in the ground. They also actively go underground to turn their buried eggs…but only for a moment.

WARTS UP?

Bullsh*t!
You can catch warts by touching a frog or a toad.

Truth:
The bumps on frogs and toads aren't even warts. And besides, the humans-only human papilloma virus spreads human warts.

JUST CHATTING

Bullsh*t!
Wolves howl at the moon.

Truth:
Wolves howl to talk to other wolves.

NO, SWEAT

Bullsh*t!

Dogs sweat by panting and salivating.

Truth:

Dogs sweat mostly through glands in their footpads. They regulate their body temperature by panting.

RUFF STUFF

Bullsh*t!

One "human year" equals seven "dog years."

Truth:

That's the result of some loose math that took the average human lifespan and equated it with the lifespan of dogs. The reasoning: If humans can live to be 100, then dogs who live to be 1/7th of that, or 14, live to be "100" in their own way. It doesn't hold up because different breeds of dog have different lifespans, ranging roughly from 9 to 16 years.

IT TAKES A LICKING

Bullsh*t!
A dog's mouth is sterile.

Truth:
Your dog's mouth is just as bacteria-laden as yours.

JUST FOR KICKS

Bullsh*t!
When you pet a dog in that certain spot and they start kicking, it's because they like it.

Truth:
That's an involuntary reaction—you've excited a nerve. And your dog hates it.

PURR-FACT!

Bullsh*t!

Cats purr when they're happy.

Truth:

Cats purr when they're happy, to communicate with their kittens, when they're sick, when they're threatened, or to calm themselves.

IF A BLACK CAT CROSSES YOUR PATH

Bullsh*t!

Panthers are a type of wild cat.

Truth:

Panthers found in Asia and Africa are a variant of leopards, and panthers found in America are a kind of jaguar.

LET IN SOME LIGHT

Bullsh*t!

Cats can see in the dark.

Truth:

Due to their curved corneas and large lenses, cats can see clearly with only 1/6th of the light that humans need.

PLAIN AND TRUE

*Bullsh*t!*
The lion is the "king of the jungle."

Truth:
Lions live in the plains.

END OF THE LINE

*Bullsh*t!*
Elephants can sense their death coming and leave their herd to instinctively find an "elephant graveyard" to join their ancestors.

Truth:
Elephants have been studied to show interest when coming across dead elephants, but they don't magically know where to go to die.

EEK!

*Bullsh*t!*
Elephants are afraid of mice.

Truth:
Elephants are very prone to getting startled by quick, sudden movements, like those of a mouse. But they're not afraid of them.

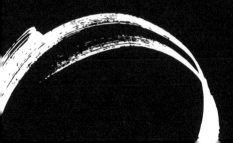

IF YOUR FRIENDS JUMPED OFF A CLIFF...

*Bullsh*t!*

Like a fatal game of "follow the leader," lemmings will march off the edge of a cliff to their deaths, one right after the other.

Truth:

People largely believe this because of a scene in the 1958 Disney nature documentary *White Wilderness*, in which filmmakers staged the shot of falling lemmings.

TRY TO BLEND IN

*Bullsh*t!*

Chameleons change color to disappear into their surroundings and avoid predators.

Truth:

Some breeds' appearance changes with the temperature or due to stress, while others may alter their color to signal to other chameleons of an imminent danger.

MONKEY SEE, MONKEY DO

*Bullsh*t!*

Primates pick at each other and eat the bugs and lice they find.

Truth:

They're picking off chunks of dead skin...and eating them.

MONKEY'S UNCLE

Bullsh*t!
Humans evolved from chimpanzees.

Truth:
The scientific consensus is that humans and chimpanzees both evolved, separately, from a common ancestor.

EVERYBODY DOES IT

Bullsh*t!
Humans are the only animals that have recreational sex.

Truth:
So do gorillas, chimpanzees, orangutans, macaques, and dolphins.

LEADER OF THE PACK

Bullsh*t!
Every wolf pack has an "alpha."

Truth:
The studies that perpetuated this fact were conducted on non-related wolves in captivity. Out in the wild, wolf packs don't appear to operate with any kind of rank, nor do young wolves overthrow the old wolves to become a new alpha.

CAN YOU BEAR IT?

Bullsh*t!
Koalas are bears.

Truth:
Koalas are marsupials and are not related to bears.

THE TRUTH IS
BLACK AND WHITE

Bullsh*t!
Pandas are bears.

Truth:
They *look* like bears, with the large bodies, big heads, and cute little ears on top of those big heads. But they're not bears; they're members of the raccoon family.

SMELL YOU LATER

Bullsh*t!
Sharks can smell blood from a mile away.

Truth:
They've got a great sense of smell, but it only covers about a quarter of a mile, tops.

JAWS 5: SHY JAWS

*Bullsh*t!*
Sharks are vicious, human-hunting monsters.

Truth:
Sharks actively keep their distance from people. More often than not, when a shark attacks a person, it's because that individual had the bad luck to hit the water right where a shark was already swimming, causing the startled shark to act defensively.

GONE FISHING

*Bullsh*t!*
Dolphins, whales, and other big sea animals drink ocean water.

Truth:
They get the water they need to live from the food they eat.

THE AIR UP THERE

*Bullsh*t!*
Whales spout water out of their blowholes.

Truth:
When a whale surfaces to breathe, it opens its blowhole, violently spewing out a bunch of moist air that was caught in there, resulting in a propelled spray that just looks like it's all water.

EIGHT IS GREAT

Bullsh*t!
Octopi have eight tentacles.

Truth:
Squids have tentacles. Octopi have arms.

THE TOOTH CAN HURT

Bullsh*t!
That appendage on the head of a narwhal is a tusk.

Truth:
It's a tooth.

DON'T SCREAM

Bullsh*t!
When plunged into boiling water to be killed and cooked, lobsters scream.

Truth:
Lobsters can't scream because they don't have vocal cords. The high-pitched sound coming from a cooking lobster are air bubbles in the shell escaping.

REMEMBER WHEN?

Bullsh*t!
Goldfish have a three-second memory span.

Truth:
Studies show that goldfish have a memory that goes back a few months.

FANGS A LOT

Bullsh*t!
Dangerous snakes are dangerous because they're poisonous.

Truth:
Dangerous snakes are venomous. Poisonous organisms spread their nastiness passively by being touched, while venomous creatures attack others to spread their stuff, which means they generally need a way to get their venom into their victims, such as fangs.

NOT SO CHARMING

Bullsh*t!
Snake charmers hypnotize snakes with their music.

Truth:
Snakes are reacting to the wind coming out of their handler's pipe.

LITTLE VAMPIRES

Bullsh*t!
Mosquitos bite.

Truth:
They don't even have teeth. They puncture the skin with a needle-like proboscis.

THE ULTIMATE ONE NIGHT STAND

Bullsh*t!
Female praying mantises eat their mates during sex.

Truth:
In controlled laboratory settings, the males ate the females just as much as the females ate the males—about 2 percent of the time.

GOT THEIR WINGS

Bullsh*t!
Bees are so light that their ability to fly violates the laws of physics.

Truth:
Scientists have figured out how bees fly; they just fly in a different manner than do other flying organisms.

WAIT A TICK

Bullsh*t!
Ticks are insects.

Truth:
Because they have four pairs of legs and no antennae, they're arachnids.

YOU DIDN'T SPY A SPIDER

Bullsh*t!
Daddy long legs are a type of spider.

Truth:
They're arachnids, but they're not spiders.

DIDN'T SEE
THIS ONE COMING

Bullsh*t!
Bats are blind.

Truth:
The vast majority of bat species navigate by echolocation, but they still have fully functional eyes.

BUGGING OUT

Bullsh*t!
Cockroaches would survive nuclear Armageddon.

Truth:
Cockroaches anywhere near the impact zone of a nuclear blast would die.

HOW TO MAKE WORMS

Bullsh*t!
Cut an earthworm in two, and it will become two new worms.

Truth:
The part with the mouth on it can continue to eat, and thus live, while the other end will quickly die.

FLY AWAY

Bullsh*t!
Never touch a butterfly, because you can easily rub off that powder on their wings, and then they won't be able to fly.

Truth:
That powder is scales, but those have nothing to do with flight. If you touch and ground a butterfly, it's because you broke one of their delicate wings.

EGG-CELLENT

Bullsh*t!

Earwigs can and will burrow into your ear and lay eggs.

Truth:

They don't do that, and the myth probably started because these critters smell like earwax. An earwig (or any other bug) couldn't be able to get that far into the ear canal before they'd reach a dead end…and then turn around and leave.

ALMOST ALL THE WAY

Bullsh*t!

Owls can spin their heads all the way around.

Truth:

Great horned owls can spin their necks 270 degrees—which is three-quarters of a full turn.

LOTS OF TIME

Bullsh*t!

Flies live only for 24 hours.

Truth:

Their lifespan is closer to 24 days.

SKUNK STUNK

Bullsh*t!
Tomato juice kills the lingering odor of skunk spray.

Truth:
It doesn't kill the smell—it just overpowers it.

CHEESY DOES IT

Bullsh*t!
Mice love cheese.

Truth:
Mice are scavengers, so they'll eat anything. They prefer sugary foods, but cheese is traditionally the bait of choice for mousetraps because it smells, thus attracting mice.

NOT ALL IT'S QUACKED UP TO BE

Bullsh*t!
A duck's quack doesn't echo.

Truth:
They do, but it's hard for the human ear to pick up on.

OH BABY

Bullsh*t!
If you touch a baby bird, the mother will abandon it.

Truth:
Birds' sense of smell isn't particularly strong, so they won't much care about your scent. It's not a good idea to handle baby birds because you can spread (or pick up) germs.

THINGS HAVE CHANGED

Bullsh*t!
The dinosaurs all went extinct at the same time.

Truth:
Many species evolved into birds.

THEY NEVER SAW A DINOSAUR

Bullsh*t!
Humans and dinosaurs walked the earth at the same time.

Truth:
While 40 percent of American adults think this is true, dinos and people missed each other by about 64 million years.

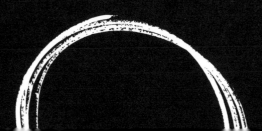

REX SPECS

Bullsh*t!

A *Tyrannosaurus rex*'s vision was based on movement.

Truth:

That's a myth propagated by *Jurassic Park*. The king of the dinosaurs had excellent vision, akin to that of a hawk, and certainly better than that of a human being.

POLLINATION CELEBRATION

Bullsh*t!

Almost all plant life on earth depends on bees for pollination, meaning humanity depends on bees for most of its food.

Truth:

Bees pollinate about 40 percent of plants consumed by humans.

GO WEST

Bullsh*t!

Tumbleweeds are native to the western United States.

Truth:

While they rolled past the screen in countless movie westerns, they're an invasive species that arrived in contaminated packages of flax seeds brought by Ukrainian immigrants to South Dakota in the late 1800s.

WHAT A REACTION

Bullsh*t!

Poison ivy is poisonous, which is why it cause a painful, itchy rash on the skin.

Truth:

It's not poisonous—it contains allergens. Poisons are toxic to all people, but allergens only get a reaction out of some people. Not *everyone* gets that nasty itch after touching this plant.

HOW STRIKING

Bullsh*t!

Lightning never strikes the same place twice.

Truth:

If a certain area is prone to thunderstorms, then lightning will eventually hit the same spot. For example, the Empire State Building endures 100 lightning strikes every year.

HERE COMES THE RAIN

Bullsh*t!

Raindrops are tear-shaped.

Truth:

They're flat, wide, and domed, similar to the top bun of a hamburger.

STILL FLUFFY

Bullsh*t!

Clouds are weightless.

Truth:

They're much bigger than you think. The average fluffy cumulus cloud is about one square kilometer in size, with a volume of a billion cubic meters. That adds up to a weight of more than one million pounds.

LATE NIGHT

Bullsh*t!

It's darkest before dawn.

Truth:

That's more of a metaphorical adage about hitting rock bottom before things improve. Astronomically speaking, it's darkest around 2 a.m.

BRIGHT AND SHINY

Bullsh*t!

Diamonds are made from coal under intense pressure.

Truth:

Diamonds are made from carbon.

RED THIS BEFORE?

Bullsh*t!
Rubies are a distinct kind of precious gem.

Truth:
They're just red sapphires (which are usually blue).

PROVE IT

Bullsh*t!
Calling it the theory of evolution means that it's just an idea—that there's some doubt.

Truth:
In the world of science, theory doesn't mean "idea." It's more akin to a thesis statement, provable with observable phenomena in the natural world. In this regard, a scientific theory is the same thing as a scientific fact.

LIFE ITSELF

Bullsh*t!
The theory of evolution explains the origin of life on Earth.

Truth:
It explains how organisms developed and changed.

WEIRD SCIENCE

Bullsh*t!

The Higgs boson particle is nicknamed the "God Particle" because it helps explain all of existence.

Truth:

The Higgs boson helped scientists better understand the structure of matter, but unlocking its secrets was so frustrating that it earned the nickname "G****** Particle," but a publisher of an important book about the concept wouldn't allow publish a book called *The G****** Particle*, so they shortened it.

STRAIGHT STORY

Bullsh*t!

There are no straight lines in nature.

Truth:

Of course there are, like in crystal formations and in snowflakes.

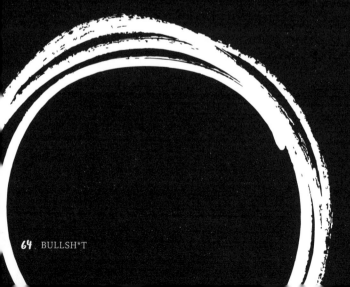

COLORS THEIR WORLD

Bullsh*t!
Dogs see in black and white.

Truth:
No, but they are quite colorblind. They see the world in shades of yellow, blue, and gray.

LAP IT UP

Bullsh*t!
Cats should drink milk.

Truth:
They'll drink it because it tastes good, but they shouldn't touch it because they're lactose intolerant, as far as cow's milk is concerned.

Are Piranhas Really *That* Flesh-Crazed?

So, piranhas are bloodthirsty monsters who will attack humans unprovoked. Not at all. In 1913, former president and adventure celebrity Teddy Roosevelt took a trip to Brazil, where locals introduced him to a river they said was full of dangerous man-eating piranhas. They threw in a bunch of raw meat, and the piranhas excitedly and violently ate it all up. Roosevelt went home and wrote extensively about his encounter with piranhas, solidifying their reputation. What he didn't know: The locals had staged the whole thing. They stocked the river beforehand with piranhas, and then starved them, ensuring they'd put on a show for their distinguished guest.

Chapter 4

Nourishing, Nourishing Knowledge

Feast on this chapter that debunks every falsehood you've ever eaten up about food.

A CREAMY FILLING
MADE OF LIES

Bullsh*t!

Twinkies last forever.

Truth:

Twinkies were one of the first mass-produced, widely distributed, preservative-packed, shelf-stable foods, leading to the notion that they'd somehow last indefinitely. The real food in Twinkies makes them semi-perishable. One stays fresh for about 45 days.

THREE-IN-ONE

Bullsh*t!

Neapolitan ice cream consists of three flavors: chocolate, vanilla, and strawberry.

Truth:

When it was introduced in Italy in the 19th century, it was meant to evoke the three colors of the Italian flag: red, white, and green. The flavors used were cherry, vanilla, and pistachio.

PIG OUT

Bullsh*t!

Eating raw or undercooked pork can make you sick.

Truth:

Pork can be infected with parasites that cause trichinosis, but modern American meat-processing techniques and laws make that far less likely now than it was even a few decades ago.

RIGHT IN THE MIDDLE

Bullsh*t!

The sandwich was invented in the 18th century, when John Montagu, the Earl of Sandwich, and an avid gambler, didn't want to leave the card table, so he asked for someone to bring him meat between two slices of bread.

Truth:

Montagu really did popularize the dish named after his title in London high society, but there's no way no one else on Earth thought of putting meat between two pieces of bread until the late 18th century. In fact, Montagu probably got the idea when he took a trip to Greece and Turkey, where he feasted on meats and cheeses placed between layers of flatbread.

BLOODY WELL RIGHT

Bullsh*t!

A slab of juicy, rare-cooked beef will let out a little blood.

Truth:

That red stuff is myoglobin, a purple-colored protein found in beef tissue, meeting oxygen, which turns it red.

A JUICY ONE

Bullsh*t!

Searing meat seals in the juices.

Truth:

Searing meat can provide a nice crust, but all methods of cooking meat lead to at least some loss of liquid.

MYSTERY MEAT

Bullsh*t!

Spam is made from, well, who even knows?

Truth:

Hormel created the product to deal with a surplus of pork shoulder. That's the main ingredient, along with ham, salt, spices, and preservatives.

MEAT CUTE

Bullsh*t!
Placing a raw steak on a black eye will help it heal.

Truth:
The cold meat may feel nice, but it won't help it heal. In fact, meat-borne illnesses like *E. coli* can spread to the eye and cause an infection.

RABBIT FOOD

Bullsh*t!
Eating lots of carrots will improve your eyesight.

Truth:
The beta carotene in carrots is good for eye health, but eating them doesn't enhance vision any.

CAKE WALK

Bullsh*t!
German chocolate cake is a German dessert.

Truth:
It used to be called German's chocolate cake, and it was the invention of an American baker named Samuel German.

REAL AMERICAN

Bullsh*t!
The chimichanga is a Mexican food.

Truth:
This deep-fried burrito was invented in Arizona.

WELL BREAD

Bullsh*t!
Croissants come from France.

Truth:
Croissants come from Austria.

FRIES LIES

Bullsh*t!
French fries are from France.

Truth:
"French" refers to the way the potato is cut into long, thin strips. The dish originated in Belgium.

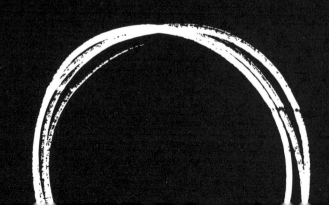

YOU WILL LEARN AN INTERESTING FACT TODAY

Bullsh*t!

Fortune cookies are Chinese.

Truth:

They were invented in San Francisco by a Japanese man.

HAIL CAESAR

Bullsh*t!

The Caesar salad is named after Julius Caesar.

Truth:

Italian cook Caesar Cardini invented it at a restaurant in Tijuana, Mexico.

LOAFING AROUND

Bullsh*t!

Pumpernickel got its name when Napoleon tasted some dark bread and thought it more suitable for his horse, Nicol. Bread for Nicol, or *pain pour nicol*, became pumpernickel.

Truth:

The word was in the German language for more than 100 years before Napoleon was born—it's an idiom that means "jerk."

FRESH MEAT

Bullsh*t!

Barbecue-style cooking was made in the U.S.A.

Truth:

It's from Barbados. Spanish explorers called the indigenous method of slow-cooking meat *barbacoa,* and brought it to what would become the U.S. when their travels took them there.

AS ENGLISH AS APPLE PIE

Bullsh*t!

Apple pie is an American invention.

Truth:

There's a recipe for a dessert consisting of a pastry shell filled with apples in a cookbook dating to 1390s England.

WHAT A CHICKEN

Bullsh*t!

The chicken chain Popeye's is named after Popeye the Sailor.

Truth:

It's named after Jimmy "Popeye" Doyle, the police detective portrayed by Gene Hackman in *The French Connection.*

BEEFING UP

Bullsh*t!

Corned beef and cabbage is a traditional Irish meal.

Truth:

When large numbers of Irish immigrants settled in New York City in the late 19th century, they bought food at delis run by Jewish immigrants. Corned beef is a dietary staple in that culture, and the Irish-Americans liked it, too.

SHAKE IT

Bullsh*t!

Ray Kroc was the founder of McDonald's.

Truth:

Dick and Mac McDonald opened the first McDonald's restaurant, a barbecue joint, in 1940. By 1954, they'd moved to selling only burgers, fries, and milkshakes and had developed a unique series of methods to cook and serve it all fast in more than 20 franchised locations. Ray Kroc, a milkshake mixer salesman, called on a McDonald's one day, got involved in the company, and bought McDonald's outright in 1961. Then he started building it into a massive worldwide operation.

HOT STUFF

Bullsh*t!

A chipotle is a certain kind of pepper.

Truth:

A chipotle is a smoked jalapeño.

A HILL OF BEANS

Bullsh*t!
Peanuts are nuts.

Truth:
They're legumes, like beans and lentils.

WORKING FOR PEANUTS

Bullsh*t!
George Washington Carver invented peanut butter.

Truth:
He devised 300 different items out of nuts, but peanut butter predated him.

RICE IS NICE

Bullsh*t!
Sushi is raw fish.

Truth:
Sushi can be made with raw or cooked fish, but the word itself refers to the vinegar-prepared rice that goes with the fish.

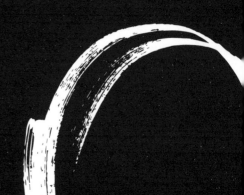

CIDER OUTSIDER

Bullsh*t!

Johnny Appleseed planted countless trees so people could have apples to eat.

Truth:

The drinking water supply in many parts of the country was subpar, and people stayed hydrated with cider—the brewing process tends to kill most water-borne germs. John "Johnny Appleseed" Chapman planted those trees not for food, but to provide apples for cider.

BRAIN DRAIN

Bullsh*t!

Drinking alcohol kills brain cells.

Truth:

Heavy drinking over a long period of time can cause brain damage, as well as damage to the liver, but that's not cell death. Thus, a drink doesn't immediately kill brain cells after it's been consumed.

WARM UPS

Bullsh*t!

Alcohol warms you up.

Truth:

It makes capillaries just under the surface of the skin dilate, increasing the amount of blood that comes to the fore, which makes you feel warm. But it doesn't change your body temperature any.

RHYME CRIME

Bullsh*t!

"Beer before liquor, never be sicker. Liquor before beer, you're in the clear."

Truth:

The order in which you drink your drinks doesn't reduce the chance of hangover or its severity.

COOK OUT

Bullsh*t!

Alcohol used in making food "cooks off" and isn't intoxicating.

Truth:

Not entirely. After an hour of cooking, 25 percent of the alcohol is intact, and after more than two hours, 5 percent remains.

MIXING IT UP

Bullsh*t!

Cocktails—alcohol mixed with juices and flavoring agents—were created during Prohibition to mask the terrible taste of rough, homemade booze or moonshine.

Truth:

As long as there has been alcohol (thousands of years), people have been mixing it with other things to make it taste better, or to dilute the alcohol, or to stretch their supply.

BUT THERE'S NO SONG CALLED "MEZCAL"

Bullsh*t!

Bottles of tequila have a worm at the bottom.

Truth:

Both tequila and mezcal are made from the agave plant, which is home to a species of moth larvae. In their worm state, that larvae are packaged in bottles of mezcal, not tequila.

GOING GREEN

Bullsh*t!

As it's made with wormwood, the green-tinted alcohol absinthe is hallucinogenic.

Truth:

It's merely a very, very strong alcoholic spirit.

MOISTURE IS MOISTURE

Bullsh*t!

Caffeine dehydrates you.

Truth:

Drinking caffeinated beverages doesn't make you expel any more water than you normally would.

HAVE A CUP WITH THE KIDS

Bullsh*t!
Coffee stunts growth.

Truth:
It's an old wives' tale.

MSGEE WHIZ

Bullsh*t!
The use of MSG in Chinese food can cause headaches and sickness.

Truth:
Monosodium glutamate is a flavor enhancer that doesn't make anybody ill. If you don't feel well after a large meal at an American-style Chinese restaurant, it's probably because you just ate a gut bomb of carbs, sugar, fat, and calories.

STILL HEALTHY

Bullsh*t!
Vegetables are a specific type of naturally growing food.

Truth:
There's no specific classification that makes a plant a "vegetable."

BAD TASTE

Bullsh*t!

In medieval times, the main use of spices in European cooking was to mask the nasty taste of rotten meat.

Truth:

Spices were used to help preserve meat, not to overpower the smell and taste of meat that had turned.

VERY SPICY

Bullsh*t!

Allspice is a mixture of various ground-up spices.

Truth:

Allspice is made from the berries of an allspice tree.

SOME LIKE IT HOT

Bullsh*t!

Eating spicy foods can cause an ulcer.

Truth:

They may exacerbate an existing ulcer, but the consumption of spicy foods can't create one.

GROUND RULE

Bullsh*t!

It's safe to eat food that's dropped on the ground if you pick it up within five seconds.

Truth:

The "five-second rule" is nonsense. Bacteria can latch onto food instantly.

SNOT A PROBLEM

Bullsh*t!

Avoid milk and dairy products when you have a cold, because it makes the body create more mucus.

Truth:

Drinking milk doesn't lead to an increase in mucus production.

FEEL THE BURN

Bullsh*t!

It takes more calories to digest a celery stalk than there are in that celery.

Truth:

A celery stalk has about six calories, and the body burns about 0.5 calories processing it.

AGING NICELY

Bullsh*t!
Wines get better with time.

Truth:
More than 90 percent of wines lose their flavor after a maximum of two years in the bottle. Heavy reds are about the only wines that do get better the longer they sit, because bitter-tasting chemicals dissipate. But after about 10 years of sitting around, little more additional change occurs.

GETTING WILD

Bullsh*t!
Wild rice is a type of rice.

Truth:
Wild rice is *Zizania aquatica*, a variety of grass seed. And while it does grow naturally, the kind they sell in stores is cultivated on large farms.

A WEIGHTY FACT

Bullsh*t!
Heavy cream is the most leaden of dairy products.

Truth:
"Heavy" means "highest fat content."

SOFT NEWS

Bullsh*t!
U.K. prime minister Margaret Thatcher invented soft-serve ice cream.

Truth:
Long before her political career, Thatcher worked as a chemist at food company J. Lyons and Co. at a time when the company was working on a new soft-serve ice cream product.

FOR KEEPS

Bullsh*t!
Never put bananas in the refrigerator.

Truth:
That's just according to the Chiquita banana commercial jingle. Keeping them on the counter until they've ripened, and *then* refrigerating them, will make them last longer.

RISE AND SHINE

Bullsh*t!
Breakfast is the most important meal of the day.

Truth:
In the 1940s and 1950s, cereal producers began fortifying their products with vitamins, and their ad campaigns used that in marketing campaigns to argue for the nutritional importance of breakfast. As far as dietary science is concerned, breakfast isn't any more vital than any other meal.

FEELING SALTY

Bullsh*t!

Need water to boil faster? Sprinkle some salt in there to speed up the process.

Truth:

Adding salt to fresh water makes no noticeable difference in the length of time it takes water to boil.

THE MAYO WAY-O

Bullsh*t!

Don't eat foods with mayonnaise in them that have been left out in the sun... unless you want to get *really* sick.

Truth:

That did used to happen, but back when people made their own mayonnaise at home. Today's packaged mayonnaises are loaded with preservatives.

On Mixing Pop Rocks and Soda

General Foods was battling "exploded kid" rumors as early as 1979, a scant four years after it introduced Pop Rocks to the marketplace. They took out full-page ads in dozens of publications, wrote 50,000 letters to schools around the country, and sent the candy's inventor on a lecture circuit to explain that Pop Rocks aren't dangerous. Pop Rocks generate less gas than a can of soda, and the only explosive reaction they can cause, even if consumed with a Coke, is a belch. Despite all that, the rumors abound that the child actor who played "Mikey" in ads for Life cereal in the early 1970s died after consuming the supposedly dangerous concoction. (He didn't.)

Chapter 5

Long Ago and So Not True

They say that the victors write history...
and they tended to fudge the details.

ROUND HERE

Bullsh*t!

Christopher Columbus sailed the ocean blue in the year 1492 to prove that the world was round.

Truth:

The Earth's roundness was general knowledge at least as far back as ancient Greece (the 3rd century B.C.). Columbus sailed west (and into America) because he was looking for a better trade route to Asia.

A LITTLE BIT OF TRUTH

Bullsh*t!

Napoleon Bonaparte was extremely short.

Truth:

Napoleon surrounded himself with his Imperial Guard, all of whom were very tall, so as to appear imposing on the battlefield. That made the emperor seem shorter than he was. Math helped, too. At the time of his death in 1821, his height was recorded as 5'2", but that's in the French measurement system of the era. In English measurements, he was 5'7", average height for a 19th-century French guy.

ARGH YOU SERIOUS?

Bullsh*t!

Pirates hit the high seas to relieve passing ships of their precious gold.

Truth:

Only movie pirates steal treasure chests full of gold doubloons. Actual pirates didn't steal much gold, as it wasn't transported via transoceanic ships. But expensive and valuable spices were, which is what pirates were really after.

THERE'S NO PLACE LIKE ROME

Bullsh*t!

Big public spaces in Ancient Rome were fitted with *vomitoria*, channels where heavily eating and drinking Romans could vomit their guts up and keep on partying.

Truth:

While Roman parties were certainly decadent bacchanals of eating and drinking, they didn't just puke their guts out in front of everybody. A *vomitorium* is a passageway surrounding a large space (such as the Colosseum) where crowds would enter and exit. The word comes from the Latin verb *vomitum*, which means "to spew."

HUMBLE BEGINNINGS

Bullsh*t!

Even geniuses stumble—after all, Albert Einstein failed math as a kid.

Truth:

He failed the math-loaded entrance exam for Zurich Polytechnic. However, he took that test two years early, and it was in French, a language in which Einstein wasn't fluent. On his second attempt, he passed.

THE NUCLEAR OPTION

Bullsh*t!

Albert Einstein helped devise the atomic bomb.

Truth:

After hearing that Nazi scientists had learned the basics of weaponized uranium, Einstein was terrified and wrote a letter to President Franklin Roosevelt in 1939, urging him to develop nuclear bombs before Hitler could. The Manhattan Project got started, but Einstein wasn't a part of it. Because of his socialist politics, he couldn't get the necessary security clearances.

STAGING A MYTH

Bullsh*t!

Vikings wore horned helmets.

Truth:

Vikings wore helmets, but the first Vikings to wear helmets with horns on them were the actors in an 1876 production of Richard Wagner's Viking-themed opera *The Ring*.

NOT A STAR

Bullsh*t!

To complicate and throw off Nazi attempts to identify Jewish people in occupied Denmark, Danish leader King Christian X wore a Jewish-identifying yellow star.

Truth:

The Danish resistance movement helped most Danish Jews safely get out of the country. But the Nazi "labeling" program was never enacted in Denmark, and so King Christian X never tried to mess with it.

BIG BUDDHA

Bullsh*t!

Buddha was an extremely heavy-set individual.

Truth:

The real name of the spiritual icon is Siddhartha Guatama, and he was very thin. Over the years, the man called the *Buddha* became confused and conflated with *Budai*, a 10th-century Chinese folk hero...and an important figure in Buddhism. All those statues and paintings depicting an overweight Buddha are actually of Budai, who was a bit rotund.

LADY OF THE NIGHT

Bullsh*t!

Jesus's good friend and follower Mary Magdalene was a prostitute.

Truth:

There are a lot of women in the Bible named Mary, and a prostitute or two. The Bible was compiled by many different writers over several centuries, and over time, the Marys got mixed up.

TRAINING REGIMEN

Bullsh*t!
Say what you will about fascist Italian dictator Benito Mussolini, but he at least "made the trains run on time."

Truth:
While that idea is primarily propaganda, Italy underwent a massive infrastructure overhaul a few years before Mussolini came into power in 1922, so things were running smoothly at that point.

OUTTA HERE

Bullsh*t!
Adam and Eve were expelled from the Garden of Eden for eating the forbidden fruit, an apple.

Truth:
The specific fruit isn't mentioned in the Bible—the first Hebrew texts just said "fruit." Early Latin translations, however, used *mali*, a word that means apple.

DON'T CALL ME THAT

Bullsh*t!
Columbus reached the New World in 1492 via a trio of ships: the *Niña*, the *Pinta*, and the *Santa Maria*.

Truth:
Two of those were the nicknames sailors had for the boats. The *Pinta* was called the *Pinta*, but the real names of the *Niña* and *Santa Maria*, respectively, were the *Santa Clara* and *La Gallega*.

MAKES SENSE

Bullsh*t!

Iceland was so named to discouragement settlement.

Truth:

There's lots of snow and ice on the island—which is why Vikings named it what they named it.

PURE TORTURE

Bullsh*t!

The iron maiden is an especially brutal medieval torture device.

Truth:

A museum put together a bunch of medieval artifacts to create one...in the 18th century.

COVER UP

Bullsh*t!

People living in repressed, conservative Victorian England thought even table and piano legs were too suggestive, so they covered them up with extra-long tablecloths.

Truth:

Victorians, especially upper-crust Victorians, liked fancy embellishments and unnecessary decorations. So while many people probably did cover up their table legs, it was a matter of taste rather than one of propriety.

FIDDLE STICKS

Bullsh*t!
Emperor Nero fiddled while Rome burned.

Truth:
The fiddle wasn't invented until about 1,000 years after Nero's death.

YAR, IT BE FALSE!

Bullsh*t!
Pirates spoke in a particular brogue.

Truth:
Englishman Robert Newton played a pirate in the 1950 film version of Robert Louis Stevenson's *Treasure Island*. His character was from southwestern England, so Newton just spoke in an exaggerated version of his own accent, giving the world the pirate. And since real pirates came from all over the world, there's no universal pirate "accent."

PATCHING THINGS UP

Bullsh*t!
Pirates wore eyepatches to cover up the unsightly eye sockets left empty due to pirating injuries.

Truth:
They wore them to be able to quickly adjust to the light or darkness from running up and down a ship's different decks.

ALWAYS BET ON BLUE

Bullsh*t!

Ninjas wore black, so as to move through the night undetected.

Truth:

The night sky isn't black—it's a very dark blue. Ninjas dressed accordingly.

HORSING AROUND

Bullsh*t!

Catherine the Great was crushed to death in 1767 when a harness holding a horse—in her bedchamber—broke.

Truth:

The Russian empress's voracious sexual appetite was well documented. She took dozens of lovers, some of whom she appointed to posts in her government. That behavior made Catherine less than popular, so it didn't take much for her people to make up, spread, and believe a rumor that exaggerated her carnal activities.

WHITE OUT

Bullsh*t!

Buildings and statues in ancient Greece and ancient Rome were white.

Truth:

They're white *now*. Those structures were initially painted all kinds of colors with natural pigments, which faded away over the centuries.

GROUP EFFORT

Bullsh*t!
Slaves built the Great Pyramids of Egypt.

Truth:
Egyptologists say they were built by Egyptian peasants, displaced by a series of floods and unable to engage in their regular work of growing crops.

HOT OFF THE PRESSES

Bullsh*t!
Johannes Gutenberg invented the printing press.

Truth:
The Gutenberg Bible was the first mass-produced printed book, but it wasn't the first printed book. Inventors in China and Korea started printing books utilizing woodblocks as a kind of movable type around 600 years before Gutenberg cobbled together his press in the 1440s.

FOUR KINGS

Bullsh*t!
Each king in a standard deck of cards represents a different king from long ago: Alexander the Great, Julius Caesar, the Biblical King David, and Charlemagne.

Truth:
The design of playing cards developed over many centuries with influences from throughout Europe, India, and China. There's no single creator of the cards, and thus no specific meaning behind the imagery.

ANOTHER ONE DOWN

Bullsh*t!

Gladiators in ancient Rome fought to the death.

Truth:

Gladiators were the sports superstars of their day, and it would have been silly for combat organizers to let their big names die every single day. Gladiator matches ended with a decisive outcome, but rarely the death of a combatant.

NOT AS BAD AS PREVIOUSLY THOUGHT

Bullsh*t!

The Spanish Inquisition unfairly tried, convicted, and executed tens of thousands of people it found to be heretics.

Truth:

In its 350 years of operation, the Spanish Inquisition returned a guilty rate of 4 percent, resulting in the deaths of about 1,800 people.

SAD, BUT TRUE

Bullsh*t!

The deadliest bombings of World War II took place when the U.S. military dropped atomic bombs on the Japanese cities of Hiroshima and Nagasaki, killing 80,000 and 75,000 people, respectively.

Truth:

On March 9, 1945, the U.S. military killed 100,000 Japanese people in a firebombing raid on Tokyo.

The Deal with Vincent Van Gogh's Ear

Did legendary French painter Vincent Van Gogh cut off his own ear and then send it to a prostitute? First of all, it would seem that his loss of an ear was an accident. On December 23, 1888, Van Gogh got into an argument with fellow artist—and accomplished fencer—Paul Gaugin...who sliced Van Gogh's ear off in a violent fit. But Van Gogh idolized Gaugin and didn't want him to get arrested, so he kept quiet and told people he cut it off himself. And while Van Gogh did send his ear to a lucky lady, she wasn't a prostitute. She was a brothel maid named Gabrielle whom Van Gogh knew had been disfigured in a dog attack, and in what was perhaps a misguided act of friendship, he sent her a piece of his own flesh to provide comfort and consolation.

Chapter 6

Places and Space

Let's take a journey to Facttown, together! (These are misconceptions about places both terrestrial and extraterrestrial.)

DUTCH TREAT

Bullsh*t!

"Holland" is another name for "the Netherlands."

Truth:

Holland *was* once its own country—about 400 years ago. Today, North Holland and South Holland are two provinces in the Netherlands.

SPEAKING ENGLISH

Bullsh*t!

Great Britain, England, and the United Kingdom all refer to the same place.

Truth:

The United Kingdom is the political entity that comprises four member nations: England, Scotland, Wales, and Northern Ireland. Great Britain is the geographical name of the landmass that contains England, Scotland, and Wales.

LONG LIVE THE KING

Bullsh*t!

The King Arthur legends are England's homegrown mythology.

Truth:

The stories date back thousands of years to folk tales from Wales and France.

A MURKY FACT

Bullsh*t!

The Everglades is a swamp.

Truth:

The Everglades is a wide, shallow, and extremely slow-moving river.

SOUTHERN COMFORT

Bullsh*t!

The southernmost U.S. state is Florida.

Truth:

It's the most southern of the states in the South, but Hawaii is at a lower latitude.

HEADED EAST

Bullsh*t!

Maine is the easternmost U.S. state.

Truth:

A few of Alaska's outermost islands sit in the Eastern Hemisphere.

TIGHTEN YOUR BELT

Bullsh*t!

The asteroid belt is densely packed with space rocks.

Truth:

On average, there's a distance of 1.2 miles between asteroids.

ROOM TO MOVE

Bullsh*t!
Alaska is the least populated U.S. state.

Truth:
Alaska has the lowest population density of all 50 states, but Wyoming has fewer total people.

STATE OF CONFUSION

Bullsh*t!
There are 50 states in the U.S.A.

Truth:
There are 46 states and four "commonwealths": Virginia, Pennsylvania, Massachusetts, and Kentucky.

CHANGE OF ADDRESS

Bullsh*t!
The Statue of Liberty is a New York landmark.

Truth:
Lady Liberty lives on Liberty Island, which sits in New York Harbor, which is inside the territorial waters of Jersey City, New Jersey.

IT'LL BLOW OVER

Bullsh*t!

Chicago is nicknamed the Windy City for all that blustery air blowing off adjacent Lake Michigan.

Truth:

The city has historically experienced so much corruption that "Windy City" refers to its blustery, blowhard local politicians.

ROLLING ON THE RIVER

Bullsh*t!

The Mississippi River is the longest river in North America.

Truth:

The Mighty Mississippi is actually about 140 miles shorter than the Missouri River.

GERM THEORY

Bullsh*t!

A toilet is the dirtiest object in the average home.

Truth:

The toilet at least gets cleaned every now and then. That's not so true for smartphones, landline phones, computer keyboards, remote controls, and doorknobs, all of which carry more germs than the commode.

SOUTHERN EXPOSURE

Bullsh*t!

Dixie is a nickname for the American South, and it's derived from the Mason-Dixon Line, the unofficial boundary that separates the South from the North.

Truth:

In the mid-1800s, Louisiana printed $10 bills emblazoned with the word *dix* (there was a large French influence in the state, and dix means "ten"). People called the bills "dixies," and the use of the word took off from there.

BY THE TIME
WE GOT TO...BETHEL?

Bullsh*t!

The legendary Woodstock concert in 1969 went down in Woodstock, New York.

Truth:

It happened at Max Yasgur's farm in Bethel, New York, about 40 miles away.

EXTRA TIME

Bullsh*t!

Daylight Saving Time was enacted to give farmers extra time to work the fields, and thus produce more food and earn more money.

Truth:

Germany was the first nation to set back its clocks in 1916 in order to conserve the use of coal during World War I. The U.S. adopted the system two years later, and for the same reason: energy conservation.

FRESH AIR

Bullsh*t!

Forests provide the world with most of its oxygen.

Truth:

Phytoplankton, one-celled organisms that live in the ocean, generate 50 percent of the planet's oxygen supply.

MAP QUEST

Bullsh*t!

World maps provide an accurate, relative scale for the size of major landmasses.

Truth:

Sizes get distorted when mapmakers try to represent a sphere as a flat object, particularly the sizes of the areas closest to the poles. Greenland and Antarctica are both much smaller than maps make them out to be, while Africa is actually much bigger than usually represented.

ISLAND LIFE

Bullsh*t!

The island Krakatoa is east of the island Java.

Truth:

Krakatoa, East of Java is the name of a 1969 disaster movie about an 1883 volcanic eruption on the Indonesian island of Krakatoa...which is actually *west* of Java.

THE PEAK OF MISINFORMATION

Bullsh*t!

Mount Everest is the tallest mountain in the world.

Truth:

Everest has a higher altitude, but the underwater Mauna Kea is actually a taller mountain. Only a small part of it juts up out of the Pacific Ocean in the form of an island.

FOUR-IN-ONE

Bullsh*t!

There's one South Pole.

Truth:

There are four: the Geographic South Pole, the South Magnetic Pole, the Geomagnetic Pole, and the South Pole of Inaccessibility.

SPACED OUT

Bullsh*t!

The Great Wall of China is so large that it's visible from space.

Truth:

It so closely blends in with its surrounding environment that it's almost impossible to see from an orbiting spacecraft.

ANOTHER RAINY DAY

Bullsh*t!
The Amazon rainforest is the wettest place on Earth.

Truth:
Mt. Waialeale, located on the Hawaiian island of Kauai, receives more rainfall than any other location on the planet—about 500 inches a year.

NOT A CLOUD IN SIGHT

Bullsh*t!
Africa's Sahara Desert is the driest place on Earth.

Truth:
It doesn't rain much in the Sahara, but it's a rainforest compared to the Dry Valleys, a region of Antarctica that hasn't experienced precipitation of any kind in about two million years.

GRAB A PLATE

Bullsh*t!
Sicily is a part of Europe.

Truth:
Politically, it's a part of Italy, but geographically the island is part of the tectonic plate of Africa.

NOT JUST ONE

Bullsh*t!

Israel is the only Jewish state in the world.

Truth:

In eastern Russia, there's a federal subject called the Jewish Autonomous Oblast.

WITHIN RANGE

Bullsh*t!

The Andes is the world's longest mountain range.

Truth:

The Mid-Atlantic Range is about twice as long. It sits in the Atlantic Ocean, and runs from Antarctica to Iceland.

SANDY BOTTOMS

Bullsh*t!

The ocean floor is lined with sand.

Truth:

Immediately off the coast of landmasses, the ocean floor is sandy. Farther out, the makeup of the sea floor changes. In deep ocean, sand is far less prominent than thick soil, sediment, rock, minerals, and even parts of the Earth's crust.

WATER,
WATER EVERYWHERE

Bullsh*t!
Water towers store drinking water.

Truth:
Not generally. Potable water comes from waterways and reservoirs, and water towers are what provide water pressure. Huge volumes of water in water towers use gravity to force the drinkable water through municipal pipes to get to where it needs to go.

WRONG WAY

Bullsh*t!
Toilet water swirls down the drain the opposite way in the Southern Hemisphere.

Truth:
The Coriolis effect's forces work on a large scale, akin to gravity. It doesn't affect water in toilets.

BEER YOU GO

Bullsh*t!
Foster's is "Australian for beer."

Truth:
It's not an Australian brand—it's brewed in Manchester, England. It was marketed as an Australian beer in the '80s during a worldwide fascination with all things Australian, such as the movie *Crocodile Dundee* starring Paul Hogan, who also appeared in Foster's TV commercials.

REDHEAD REDEMPTION

Bullsh*t!

Redheaded Irish people are common, and redheads are usually of Irish descent.

Truth:

Only 10 percent of Irish people are carrot-tops, but 13 percent of Scottish people are.

SLEEP ON IT

Bullsh*t!

Catching a quick nap, or *siesta*, is common in Spain.

Truth:

It's fallen out of favor in modern Spain, a country that's a big player in international economics. Many businesses still close down for a couple of hours in the afternoon, but that essentially amounts to a lunch break. Some workers may utilize that time for a nap, but it's no longer culturally dominant to do so.

PARDON OUR FRENCH

Bullsh*t!

French people are rude.

Truth:

Americans visiting France may think this because of a big cultural difference—in France, directness is a virtue.

THE TOOTH OF THE MATTER

Bullsh*t!

English people have bad teeth.

Truth:

The country's National Health Service covers its citizens' medical care, but not its dental care, so for decades dentistry wasn't a priority for many. Since the 1980s, however, American-style cosmetic dentistry—orthodontics, teeth whitening—has become a regular part of life in England.

HERE COMES THE SUN

Bullsh*t!

Summer happens when the Earth, in its annual revolution around the sun, gets close to the hot star.

Truth:

Seasons are caused by the Earth's tilt on its axis, not its proximity to the sun.

THE GRAVITY OF THE SITUATION

Bullsh*t!

Black holes exert tremendous gravitational pull, aggressively sucking in anything that gets close.

Truth:

A black hole possesses the same level of gravity as another celestial body of the same size.

PINK FLOYD WAS MISTAKEN

Bullsh*t!
There's a dark side of the moon.

Truth:
There's a near side of the moon, the one that always faces the Earth due to the planet's strong gravitational pull, and there's a far side, which we humans don't see much. When the moon gets between the sun and the Earth, that far side is illuminated.

HOLDING IT DOWN

Bullsh*t!
Astronauts on space walks float around because there's no gravity in space.

Truth:
Space is full of gravity, particularly in the areas around Earth where astronauts work—that gravity is what keeps the moon in orbit. The astronauts' floating comes from being in a state of very slow freefall, not a lack of gravity.

BRIGHT AND SHINY

Bullsh*t!
The sun is yellow.

Truth:
When viewed through the Earth's atmosphere, the sun looks yellow (or orange, or red). It's actually white.

Chapter 7

Word World

What's the good word? Getting these misconceptions about language out of your mind!

THANKS, POPEYE!

Bullsh*t!

The Jeep gets its name from a full pronunciation of "GP"—the name of similar "general purpose" military vehicles used in World War II.

Truth:

Jeeps are based on GP vehicles, but the name comes from the pre-World War II *Popeye* comic strip. One of Popeye's friends was an animal of extraordinary ability named Eugene the Jeep.

A NON-STARTER

Bullsh*t!

When the Chevy Nova was introduced into Latin America, it sold poorly because in Spanish, "nova," or "no va," means "doesn't go."

Truth:

Cited as an example in numerous business textbooks as a marketing snafu or not properly researching one's audience, it's just not true. The Chevy Nova sold very well in South America, and Spanish speakers are intelligent enough to understand compound words. Also, "nova" and "no va" are pronounced differently, so there's that.

A CUT ABOVE THE REST

Bullsh*t!

The Caesarean method of baby delivery—in which a doctor surgically removes the infant from the womb—is named after Julius Caesar, the first person born in such a manner.

Truth:

Caesarean comes from the Latin word *caedere*, which means "to cut."

CODED MESSAGE

Bullsh*t!

The distress signal "S.O.S." delivered via Morse Code is an abbreviation of "save our ship."

Truth:

S.O.S. was selected as a distress signal because it's easy to remember and quick to express via telegraph: one short pulse, one long pulse, and another short pulse.

JUST YOUR TYPE

Bullsh*t!

In typed documents, always leave two spaces after a period.

Truth:

When typed documents became standard operating procedure in business and government communications in the early 20th century, double-spacing was done to make the page easier to read. But years ago, all three major English language guides—The A.P. Stylebook, the Chicago Manual of Style, and the U.S. Government Printing Office Style Manual—got rid of this rule. One space is sufficient.

100 Words for Snow

Supposedly, the Eskimos have more than 100 words for snow, because they experience so many different types of it. First of all, there's no one people called Eskimos; Algonquin tribes in Quebec used "Eskimo" as an umbrella term for all the native groups who live in what is now Canada. When you think of an Eskimo (bundled up in a big coat, sitting by an igloo) you're probably thinking of an exaggerated version of an Inuit or Yupik person. Five major languages link these various cold-weather native groups, along with dozens of dialects and variations. So then why do people think Eskimos are a singular group with multiple words for snow? In 1911, linguist Franz Boas referred to all native Canadians as Eskimos as a whole, and wrote that they had four words for snow: *aput* (snow on the ground), *qana* (falling snow), *pigsirpoq* (drifting snow), and *qimuqsuq* (a snow drift). Linguists kept writing about this phenomenon, but increased the number of words for snow each time.

PERUSE THIS WHEN YOU GET A CHANCE

Bullsh*t!
To peruse a document means the same as skimming it or flipping through.

Truth:
It actually means the opposite—to read carefully and attentively.

WHEREFORE THIS?

Bullsh*t!
"Wherefore" means the same as "where."

Truth:
In one of the most famous passages from William Shakespeare's *Romeo and Juliet*, Juliet stands on her balcony and implores, "Romeo, Romeo, wherefore art thou, Romeo?" She's not wondering where her boyfriend is, but rather *why* he is—specifically, a Montague, one of the sworn enemies of her family, the Capulets.

STUCK IN THE BATHROOM

Bullsh*t!
"Crap" comes from Thomas Crapper, the man who invented the flush toilet.

Truth:
Thomas Crapper didn't invent the flush toilet—he was a 19th-century English plumber who ran a fixtures company and he held patents for a number of plumbing improvements. Nor did we get the semi-crude word "crap" from his name. Crap derives from the Latin word *crappa*, which means crop chaff...a form of waste material.

ORANGE YOU GLAD YOU READ THIS?

Bullsh*t!

No words rhyme with "orange."

Truth:

A *sporange* is a structure in fungi, algae, and mosses that produces spores.

WHAT TIME IS IT?

Bullsh*t!

Marijuana smokers around the world do their thing at 4:20 each day (and all day long on 4/20—April 20) because "420" is official police code for the illegal smoking of marijuana.

Truth:

In 1971, five burnouts at San Rafael High School were called the Waldos, because they liked to hang out near a wall by the school. It was by this wall that they met each day at 4:20 p.m. to smoke marijuana.

AN ARRESTING FACT

Bullsh*t!

Police officers are called cops because they used to wear uniforms with large copper buttons, prompting people to call them "coppers" (which got shortened to cops).

Truth:

Cop is a centuries-old word in English which means "to take," and in the 18th century its definition expanded to include "to arrest." Police who arrested criminals, the ones who would cop, came to be called coppers.

ARE YOU READY FOR THIS JELLY?

Bullsh*t!

In 1963, President John F. Kennedy gave a rousing speech in support of democracy. In front of a crowd in West Berlin, Kennedy remarked, in German, "Ich bin Berliner." He left out the indefinite article "ein," which means that while he intended to say "I am a Berliner" (a message of solidarity), he said "I am a jelly doughnut," as Berliner is another name for that pastry.

Truth:

It's a rumor and urban legend. Kennedy said, "Ich bin ein Berliner" in full, and to rousing applause...and no laughter.

A PLAGUE OF MISTRUTHS

Bullsh*t!

The "Ring Around the Rosie" poem is about the Black Plague. The "rings" are the black circles that appear on plague victims' skin, the "pocket full of posies" are flowers people carried to mask the smell of dead bodies everywhere," "ashes, ashes" refers to the mass incineration of dead bodies, and "we all fall down" meant that the plague hit everyone—rich or poor.

Truth:

It's an old pagan song that predates the outbreaks of the plague in the 1300s by centuries. It wasn't until 1961 in James Leasor's book *The Plague and the Fire* that anybody suggested the song contained coded messages about the devastating disease.

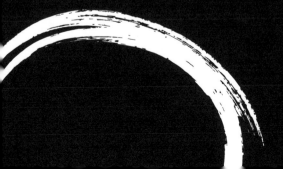

WHAT ROOM ARE YOU READING THIS IN?

Bullsh*t!

Never end a sentence with a preposition.

Truth:

There's no rule in the English language that forbids it. It also allows you to end sentences so they sound like people talk, instead of all clunky and stilted. For example, it's perfectly fine to say "Where do I come in?" as opposed to the more awkward, "In where do I come?"

HAT TIP TO THE TRUTH

Bullsh*t!

A cowboy hat is also called a "ten-gallon hat" because it can hold that much water.

Truth:

"Ten" and "gallon" are pre-existing words in the English language, but in this capacity, "ten gallon" is a corruption of a Spanish phrase. Mexican-born cowboys called their hats "tan galán," which translates to "very handsome."

WAKE UP

Bullsh*t!

Coma comes from a medical acronym ascribed to living but unconscious patients: "cessation of motor activity."

Truth:

Coma is from *koma*, a Greek word that means "an intense sleep."

TO TELL YE TRUTH

Bullsh*t!

In old-timey medieval England, they used the word "ye" (pronounced "yee") instead of "the." (As in "Ye Olde Apothecary and Surgical Barber.")

Truth:

"Ye" and "the" are the same word—pronounced the same but expressed with different letters. Before either spelling, the word was spelled *þe*. That first letter was called *thorn*, which faded out of English hundreds of years ago and provided a "th" sound. As the years wore on, the shape of þ changed so that it looked like another now disused letter, ◌, and eventually became impossible to tell apart from y.

DINOSAUR FACT

Bullsh*t!

The word dinosaur is Latin for "terrible lizard."

Truth:

Paleontologist Richard Owen coined the word in 1842, and it's based on a Greek construction that means "fearfully great lizard." And Owen meant "fearfully great" as a compliment.

WAY BACK WHEN

Bullsh*t!

The phrase "time immemorial" is synonymous with "very long ago" or "before recorded history."

Truth:

Under English law, the term refers to anything that happened before Richard the Lionheart ascended to the throne on July 6, 1189.

SPELLING TEST

Bullsh*t!
It's a steadfast spelling rule: "i" before "e," except after "c."

Truth:
The English language is full of exceptions, and this rule doesn't apply around 30 percent of the time. *Albeit*, that's some *weird science*.

DRYING OUT

Bullsh*t!
Dry cleaning is "dry" cleaning.

Truth:
Clothes are cleaned with a variety of chemicals and solvents. It's called dry cleaning because no water is used.

OH, SHIP

Bullsh*t!
The word sh*t comes from the acronym "ship high in transit," a directive placed on shipping boats containing manure. The warning would ensure proper handling so as not to waterlog the cargo on board and release noxious (and explosive) methane.

Truth:
According to linguists, sh*t comes from the Old English word *scitte*, which translates to "diarrhea" or "to purge."

AND NOW, THE NEWS

Bullsh*t!

The word "news" came about by combining the first letters of the cardinal directions: North, East, West, and South. News events thusly refer to things that happened from all over.

Truth:

News is merely the modern spelling of a word that's been variously spelled as *newesse, newis, neus, newys, newis, nues*, and more. It's actually the plural of "new" because news stories are new stories.

OH, FUDGE

Bullsh*t!

The F-word (and its use as crude way to describe the sexual act) stems from the acronym "for unlawful carnal knowledge," a charge levied when people were caught engaged in certain illegal acts.

Truth:

Linguists say it likely comes from the Dutch word *fokken*, or "to breed."

HOT FACTS HERE!

Bullsh*t!

"Selling like hotcakes" means an item is popular and selling quickly.

Truth:

"Selling like hotcakes" properly refers to something selling briskly because they're hot and fresh out of the oven or frying pan. Who would want hotcakes that weren't hot?

Famous Names You've Probably Been Mispronouncing

J.K. Rowling

The first syllable rhymes with "no," not "now."

Vincent Van Gogh

It's "van guff," not "van go."

Bjork

It's "byerk" not "byork."

Dr. Seuss

Theodore Seuss Geisel pronounced his middle/pen name as "Soyce."

Matt Groening

The first syllable sounds like "grain" instead of "groan."

Maya Angelou

Think "an-jell-oh" and not "an-jell-oo."

Shia LaBeouf

"La buff," not "la boof."

Steve Buscemi

It's "boo-sem-me" not "boo-shem-me."

Chapter 8

The Sporting Life

It's "game on" for hipping you to the real stories behind these commonly believed sports mistruths.

ROLLING ALONG

Bullsh*t!

In 1986, Bill Buckner lost the World Series for the Boston Red Sox when he allowed a hit ball to roll through his legs.

Truth:

That play happened in Game Six of the championship series against the New York Mets. The Red Sox lost that night, but they still had a chance to win in the decisive seventh game, and they didn't.

A SICK STORY

Bullsh*t!

Michael Jordan had one of the greatest nights of his career with Game 5 of the 1997 NBA Finals, putting up 38 points for the Chicago Bulls...despite having the flu.

Truth:

It's far more likely that he had food poisoning. According to Bulls trainer Tim Grover, the illness stemmed from a bad pizza Jordan ate the night before.

IT'S A MIRACLE

Bullsh*t!

The "Miracle on Ice" went down at the 1980 Winter Olympics, in which a ragtag group of American hockey players defeated the heavily favored (and hated) Soviet Union to win the gold medal.

Truth:

Yes, Team USA beat the USSR, and they won the gold medal, but the "Miracle on Ice" was a gold medal match *qualifier*. In the gold medal game, the U.S. beat Finland to win it all.

A CUT ABOVE

Bullsh*t!

Don't give up on your dreams; after all, Michael Jordan was cut from his high school basketball team.

Truth:

Jordan was a sophomore and was moved over to the junior varsity squad, so as to give a spot on the varsity team to an upperclassman.

THE LONG RUN

Bullsh*t!

The length of a marathon—26.2 miles—is based on the distance an ancient Greek solider ran from Marathon to Athens in 490 B.C. to tell the Athenians that their side had been victorious in the Battle of Marathon.

Truth:

The distance of 26.2 miles was the length of the marathon in the 1908 Summer Olympics.

BLAZING A NEW TRAIL

Bullsh*t!

The Portland Trail Blazers made the biggest draft blunder of all time in 1984, selecting Sam Bowie and allowing the Chicago Bulls, who had the next pick, to select Michael Jordan.

Truth:

The Blazers needed a center, and so they took Bowie with the #2 pick in the 1984 NBA Draft. They already had a star shooting guard in Clyde Drexler. He went on to become an Olympic gold medal-winning basketball player and member of the Naismith Memorial Basketball Hall of Fame, just like Jordan.

HEAVY METAL

Bullsh*t!
Olympic gold medals are made of gold.

Truth:
Not entirely, and barely at all. In recent years, the gold medal has been made up of 93 percent silver, 6 percent copper, and around 1 percent gold.

NO CANADA

Bullsh*t!
Hockey originated in Canada, the country that loves it the most.

Truth:
Old documents show that it was played in England at least as early as the 1850s.

BO KNOWS MISCONCEPTIONS

Bullsh*t!
Bo Jackson was the first athlete to simultaneously play pro football and big-league baseball.

Truth:
He was just the first to excel at both. The Heisman Trophy winner was an all-star in both sports and was heavily hyped by Nike's "Bo Knows" ads. Jackson was preceded in his football/baseball juggling by Christy Matthewson. The Hall of Famer pitched in the National League from 1900 to 1916, and played fullback for the Greensburg Athletic Association and the Pittsburgh Stars from 1898 through 1902.

MAY WE INJECT?

Bullsh*t!

Baseball was ruined—or at least scandalized—when it was revealed that numerous players in the 1990s and 2000s used performance-enhancing drugs.

Truth:

The Mitchell Report, which shed light on the issue in 2007, calculated that widespread steroid use began in Major League Baseball around 1973. But long before that, back in 1889, star pitcher Pud Galvin publicly credited his excellent play to the Brown-Sequard elixir, an injected concoction made from animal testosterone.

GOING STREAKING

Bullsh*t!

The first of Lou Gehrig's record-breaking, 2,130 games-played streak began when regular Yankees first basemen Wally Pipp didn't want to play because of a mild headache.

Truth:

Wally Pipp indeed gave up his spot in the lineup to Gehrig one day in 1925, but it was because he'd suffered a fractured skull in a batting practice accident.

WHAT A CHAMP!

Bullsh*t!

Racehorses ready to race are said to be "chomping at the bit."

Truth:

It's "champing" not "chomping." Champing means "grinding," which is exactly what a racehorse does with the bit in its mouth.

ONE TRUE KING

Bullsh*t!

Barry Bonds is the all-time home run king, knocking 762 out of the park.

Truth:

The National League and the American League wouldn't allow African-Americans to play in the early decades of the 20th century, leading to the development of the concurrent "Negro Leagues." One of that world's biggest stars was: power hitter Josh Gibson. While records are spotty, he reportedly hit as many as 962 home runs in his career.

TRUE PIONEERS

Bullsh*t!

African-American athlete Jackie Robinson broke the baseball color barrier when he first played for the Brooklyn Dodgers in 1947.

Truth:

The American League joined the National League as one of baseball's two "big leagues" upon its creation in 1901. Its predecessor: the American Association. In 1884, Moses Fleetwood Walker joined that league's Toledo Blue Stockings for a single season, making him the first African-American player in the big leagues.

IT AIN'T SO

Bullsh*t!

Eight players from the Chicago White Sox threw the 1919 World Series and earned lifetime bans from baseball. Among them was Shoeless Joe Jackson, who was probably not in on the fix, but was punished nonetheless. In a famous moment that became part of baseball's storied history, a little boy approached Jackson after his trial and said, "Say it ain't so, Joe, say it ain't so!"

Truth:

In 1949, Jackson told *Sport* that *Chicago Daily News* sportswriter Charley Owens had invented the exchange.

MAKE A CALL

Bullsh*t!

If in baseball a runner touches a base at exactly the same time as he's tagged out, the tie goes to the runner.

Truth:

There's nothing in the official baseball rule book that supports this. As with any call, it's up to the umpire to decide.

WRESTLE WITH THIS

Bullsh*t!

Professional wrestling is fake.

Truth:

Wrestling is anything but fake—those men and women in the WWE really do wrestle each other, and they can and do get hurt. However, it is *scripted*—outcomes are predetermined and wrestlers even work out what moves they're going to do, and in what order.

NET PROFIT

Bullsh*t!
Jay-Z owns the Brooklyn Nets.

Truth:
At one point, the rapper was part of an ownership group, and his stake in the team amounted to 1/15 of 1 percent. He sold his shares in 2013.

A MAGICAL TALE

Bullsh*t!
The Orlando Magic is named after the city's biggest attraction, Disney World, a.k.a. the "Magic Kingdom."

Truth:
The team was all set to be named the Juice, after Florida's citrus industry, until a team executive's young daughter paid a visit to Orlando and remarked, "This place is like magic!"

YOU DO THE MATH

Bullsh*t!
NBA legend Wilt "The Stilt" Chamberlain went to bed with 20,000 women.

Truth:
Chamberlain offered up this unverified factoid in his 1991 memoir *A View From Above*. While he may have gotten around, that number can only be an exaggeration. Assuming Chamberlain first became active around age 15, and hit that twenty-grand at 55 (when he wrote his book), that works out to an average of 1.4 women a day, *every* day.

EVERYBODY'S WATCHING

Bullsh*t!

The Super Bowl is the most watched sporting event in the world.

Truth:

The Olympics, the Cricket World Cup, and the FIFA World Cup of soccer all bring in around a billion viewers when they're held every four years, way more than the Super Bowl.

JOIN THE CLUB

Bullsh*t!

The word "golf" comes from an acronym when it was a men's only sport. It stands for "gentlemen only, ladies forbidden."

Truth:

It stems from a word that means "club."

JUST KICKING IT

Bullsh*t!

Americans hate soccer.

Truth:

Major League Soccer puts up attendance numbers on par with the NHL or the NBA, but even before that league exploded in popularity, Americans loved soccer—playing it, not watching it. About three million kids a year sign up for youth soccer.

Abner Doubleday, Baseball Inventor

The sport evolved out of the similar British sports of cricket and rounders, which is what *Baseball Guide* editor Henry Chadwick tried to write in 1903, until his publisher, Albert Spalding (as in Spalding sporting goods) wouldn't allow it, believing that an American game simply *must* have American origins. Spalding formed a commission, and in 1907 issued a report that concluded future Civil War general Abner Doubleday devised the basics of "base ball" in Cooperstown, New York, back in 1839. That was based almost entirely on a letter sent in by a man named Abner Graves, who said he was present that day in 1839 when Doubleday drew a diamond in a dirt field and got a game going. Spalding took Graves at his word, ignoring the fact that in 1839 Doubleday was an army cadet and nowhere near New York, or that in all of his diaries and correspondence, Doubleday never once mentioned inventing a sport. Doubleday became and remained the inventor of the national pastime in the collective mind, even after baseball commissioner Kennesaw Mountain Landis received a letter in the 1930s from a man named Bruce Cartwright with proof that his grandfather, Alexander Cartwright, invented the game. The younger man provided original written rules, a field diagram, and a scorecard from the first game played in Hoboken, New Jersey, in 1845.

Chapter 9

That's Entertainment?

In which we do some damage
control on all the things you
think you know about the
Hollywood dream factory.

SOMETHING IN THE AIR

Bullsh*t!
The word "sex" is subliminally hidden in a dust cloud in *The Lion King*.

Truth:
The word is the similar-appearing "SFX," inserted as a joke by the special effects (SFX) team who worked on the shot.

BAD KITTY

Bullsh*t!
A whispered line in *Aladdin* (1992) implores "good teenagers, take off your clothes."

Truth:
The offensive moment supposedly takes place when *Aladdin*, dressed as Prince Ali, flies on his magic carpet to Jasmine's balcony. When he gets there, her tiger, Rajah, tries to get rid of Aladdin and growls, prompting Aladdin to mutter, "Good teenagers, take off your clothes." According to Disney, however, Aladdin says, "Come on good kitty, take off and go."

HAM ON LIE

Bullsh*t!
"Mama" Cass Eliot of the Mamas and the Papas died from choking on a ham sandwich.

Truth:
The coroner's initial report, which was leaked to the media, noted that a ham sandwich was found near her body. There were no obstructions in her windpipe—an autopsy revealed that the singer died of a heart attack.

KEEPING IT IN THE FAMILY

Bullsh*t!

Woody Allen married his adopted daughter, Soon-Yi Previn.

Truth:

She's the adopted daughter of Allen's former partner (not spouse) Mia Farrow. The actress adopted her with her former husband, composer Andre Previn.

NEED A HAND?

Bullsh*t!

In the *Super Mario* video games, Mario jumps up and smashes blocks with his head.

Truth:

He's using his fist.

DISNEY ON ICE

Bullsh*t!

The body of Walt Disney (or maybe just his head) was cryogenically frozen, and when science develops the technology to revive dead people, he'll come back to life.

Truth:

The entertainment tycoon died from cancer in 1966. He was cremated two days after his death, but Bob Nelson of the Cryonics Society of California mentioned years later in an interview that Disney had shown interest in freezing his body...but died before he could make the plans to do so. That bit of info, combined with how Nelson's organization happened to freeze its first body two weeks after Disney died, became "Walt Disney is cryogenically frozen."

OH, YOKO

Bullsh*t!

Yoko Ono broke up the Beatles.

Truth:

By the time Yoko Ono and John Lennon found each other in 1968, the pressures of being in the biggest band in the world—and creative differences among the four strong-headed musicians—were already threatening to split the band apart. Yoko Ono just came around at a time when she could be a scapegoat for angry Beatles fans. In 1969, John Lennon told *NME* that he formed the Plastic Ono Band with Ono because "there isn't enough outlet for me in the Beatles."

NICE TO SEE YOU AGAIN

Bullsh*t!

The Beatles broke up in 1970 and never reunited.

Truth:

After John Lennon died in 1980, George Harrison wrote a song called "All Those Years Ago," a nostalgic tune about Beatlemania on which Paul McCartney sang backup and Ringo Starr played the drums. And in 1998, at a private memorial service for the late Linda McCartney, her husband, along with Harrison and Starr, led the congregation in the singing of "Let it Be."

A HAPPY MINISTER

Bullsh*t!
During a wedding scene in *The Little Mermaid*, the minister sports an erection.

Truth:
The minister is very short and squat, and his knee jutting out from underneath his tunic certainly made it look like a different protuberance.

SIGN HERE

Bullsh*t!
The Disney logo is Walt Disney's handwritten signature.

Truth:
The Disney corporation introduced that logo in the 1980s during a downturn, as a way to link the company back to its glory days. The "Waltograph" is a stylized, designed version of Disney's signature, but it isn't a facsimile.

DUSTING THIS ONE OFF

Bullsh*t!
Blowing into a video game cartridge clears out dust and helps it run better.

Truth:
Dust and dirt could get inside both a Nintendo Entertainment System and around the connection ports at the bottom of the game, and players blamed that when a game didn't work properly, so they'd remove it, blow on it, then put it back in. Blowing actually did nothing—it "worked" because of that mystifying technological phenomenon of "turning it off and turning it back on again."

WHAT A FOX

Bullsh*t!

Actor Michael J. Fox has a middle name that starts with the letter "J."

Truth:

His middle name is Andrew. When he joined the Screen Actors Guild, there was already a member named Michael Fox. The Canadian didn't want to use "A" as a middle initial because it sounded like the cliché Canadian expression "eh," so he adopted a "J" as a tribute to one of his acting heroes, Michael J. Pollard.

ROCK ME, AMADEUS!

Bullsh*t!

Wolfgang Amadeus Mozart and his less-talented contemporary Antonio Salieri were bitter enemies, to the point where an insanely jealous Salieri killed Mozart.

Truth:

Most everything we think we know about these two comes from the highly dramatized 1984 film *Amadeus*. Not only was Salieri a successful composer of 40 popular operas, but he and Mozart were friends and even collaborators. And Mozart died in 1791 of an illness...not murder.

CURVES AHEAD

Bullsh*t!

Marilyn Monroe was a size 16.

Truth:

Monroe did wear a size 16 in the '50s, but a size 16 back then isn't the same as a size 16 today. A past 16 is equivalent to a present-day 4.

EYE, EYE!

Bullsh*t!

Veteran TV star Sandy Duncan—*Funny Face, The Sandy Duncan Show,* and *The Hogan Family*—has a glass eye.

Truth:

In 1971, Duncan had a noncancerous tumor behind her left eye removed, but it left her blind in that eye due to a surgical complication. So while Duncan's left eye lacks a little warmth, it's because it doesn't work, not because it isn't real.

(TELE)VISIONS OF JOANNA

Bullsh*t!

Born with the name Robert Zimmerman, Bob Dylan adopted his stage name to pay tribute to Welsh writer Dylan Thomas.

Truth:

Dylan may be an artist of the highest caliber but he still loves TV like the rest of us. The "Dylan" is a conscious re-spelling of Dillon, as in Matt Dillon, a character from *Gunsmoke*.

A TALENTED KID

Bullsh*t!

Mozart wrote "Twinkle, Twinkle, Little Star" at the age of five.

Truth:

He was a child prodigy of a composer, but Wolfgang Amadeus Mozart didn't write "Twinkle, Twinkle, Little Star." At age 25, he composed *Twelve Variations on "Ah, vous dirai-je, Maman."* The basic melody was later used for "Twinkle, Twinkle, Little Star."

LIAR, BAD!

Bullsh*t!

Mary Shelley's novel *Frankenstein* and its countless film adaptations are about a fire-hating monster named Frankenstein, constructed out of dead body parts, and reanimated with a jolt of electricity.

Truth:

The novel is more about the dangers of man "playing God" than the monster's rampage. It's about Frankenstein, alright—Dr. Victor Frankenstein, the guy who builds the creature. The monster is never named.

MOVIES AREN'T REAL

Bullsh*t!

Audiences for some of the first films in the 1890s were so amazed by movies that they thought they were witnessing real events. There was even a mass panic during an 1896 showing of *Arrival of a Train at La Ciotata* when the filmgoers screamed and ran away, convinced the flickering two-dimensional train would burst through the screen.

Truth:

People can easily differentiate fiction from reality—they've been watching plays for centuries. Also, early films offered very poor resolution—and in black and white, and silent—so there's no way anybody thought that the train was real.

A TRUE CLASSIC

Bullsh*t!

Music performed by a full symphonic orchestra in a concert hall is called classical music.

Truth:

"Classical" is often used to describe any and all "fancy" instrumental music composed a couple of hundred years ago by the likes of Bach and Beethoven, but it technically refers only to a very specific era of music. "Classical" music dates to 1760-1820 (give or take), and covers the period in which Mozart, Hayden, and other composers toned down the grandiosity of the baroque period (1600 to 1760) so as to re-focus on melody.

WALL OF CONFUSION

Bullsh*t!

Germans love David Hasselhoff.

Truth:

The fall of the Berlin Wall in 1989 was a surprising event, made all the more unbelievable when Hasselhoff showed up among the rubble to perform his single "Looking for Freedom" to cheering Germans. That song was something of an unofficial theme song of the political upheaval that had led to the end of European communism, and it spent eight weeks at #1 in West Germany. Hasselhoff never had another huge hit in Germany, so no, Germans really only loved him for that one special moment in time. Most affection for Hasselhoff found in Germany today is of the kitschy or ironic variety.

JOANIE LOVES LYING

Bullsh*t!

Joanie Loves Chachi, a 1982 spinoff of *Happy Days* about young married couple Joanie Cunningham (Erin Moran) and Chachi Arcola (Scott Baio), flopped in the U.S., but was extraordinarily popular when it aired in Korea because "chachi" is Korean slang for "penis."

Truth:

This is a lie *Happy Days* and *Joanie Loves Chachi* creator Garry Marshall dropped into interviews to build up word of mouth...because there's no better publicity than a hint of sex and scandal.

THE OSCAR GOES TO...

Bullsh*t!

Marisa Tomei didn't *really* win Best Supporting Actress at the 1993 Academy Awards for her role in *My Cousin Vinny*.

Truth:

Tomei's win was certainly a surprise—prognosticators thought Judy Davis in *Husbands and Wives* was a lock. But Tomei's name is what came out of the mouth of 74-year-old presenter Jack Palance, who seemed a little confused and stumbled over his prepared remarks. Tomei's shocking win, combined with Palance's demeanor, let to a persistent rumor that Palance read the final name of the nominees on the teleprompter rather than the name of the winner in the envelope. But if there are ever errors—such as the fiasco in 2017 when *La La Land* was mistakenly announced as the Best Picture winner—someone will step in to correct things.

SHAKESPEARE IN LIMBO

Bullsh*t!

Shakespeare was the most respected writer of his time.

Truth:

Shakespeare's plays were popular entertainments in the late 15th and early 16th centuries...and almost as popular as works written by contemporaries like Ben Jonson and Christopher Marlowe. He wasn't regarded as the greatest writer in the English language until the early 1800s, when influential poet Samuel Taylor Coleridge re-popularized his works.

DEATH BED

Bullsh*t!

William Shakespeare willed to his wife, Anne Hathaway, little more than his "second-best bed." *That's* all he could give to the love of his life? What a jerk!

Truth:

Shakespeare really did leave his wife their "second-best bed." But the reason why is actually very sweet. In Elizabethan England, a home's best bed was reserved for visiting guests. The marriage bed where the man and woman of the house slept was thus the second-best. Shakespeare was giving a sexy little wink to his wife in his will, remembering all the first-rate times they had together on their second-best bed.

THE IMPORTANCE OF BEING ERNEST

Bullsh*t!

Ernest Hemingway wrote a haunting short story consisting of just six words: "For sale. Baby shoes. Never worn."

Truth:

It's a myth about Hemingway that originated in *Papa*, John deGroot's 1996 one-man show about Hemingway.

NO SALE

Bullsh*t!

Robert Johnson sold his soul to the devil in exchange for the skills that made him a master blues musician.

Truth:

It's a legend, of course, but it's been incorrectly attributed to Johnson. Another early 20th-century musician named Tommy Johnson claimed that he's the one who made the arrangement with the devil.

A GRUNGY FACT

Bullsh*t!

Nirvana killed "hair metal" when it popularized grunge music with its 1991 single "Smells Like Teen Spirit."

Truth:

The more serious hard rock of bands like Guns N' Roses and Metallica killed hair metal in the late '80s, and bands like those sold millions of records well into the '90s, alongside grunge bands like Nirvana and Pearl Jam.

THREE MEN AND A GHOST

Bullsh*t!

The ghost of a teenage boy appears in the movie *Three Men and a Baby*. When the comedy hit VHS in 1988, people started noticing—and talking about—a figure that appears in one scene. A brunette male figure appears in the background, his facial features tough to make out, peeking from behind a curtain. That led to the urban legend that it's the ghost of a boy who committed suicide in the house where the movie was filmed.

Truth:

Ted Danson plays an actor in the movie, and in a deleted scene, the audience gets a glimpse of a cardboard cutout of him wearing a tuxedo. A crew member then stashed the fake Danson behind a curtain, and when that other scene was filmed, the cutout was barely, but spookily, visible. (And *Three Men and a Baby* wasn't even filmed in a house—it was shot on a soundstage.)

BASED ON A FAKE STORY

Bullsh*t!

The 1996 Oscar-nominated movie *Fargo*, the story of a kidnapping gone wrong that ends in multiple deaths and a fortune stashed in a snowbank, is based on a true story.

Truth:

Writer-director team Joel and Ethan Coen put a "based on a true story" disclaimer at the beginning of the movie to make the film seem more visceral and shocking. But they made up the whole thing.

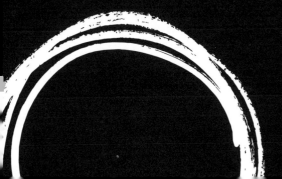

UNDERCOVER BOSS

Bullsh*t!

Steven Spielberg secretly directed the 1984 film *Poltergeist*, not credited director Tobe Hooper.

Truth:

This was the first big-budget movie Hooper, who'd gotten his start on low-budget indies like *The Texas Chainsaw Massacre*, was in charge of, so he needed some help here and there. Spielberg, *Poltergeist*'s screenwriter and producer, offered suggestions, which crew and cast members took to mean he was secretly running the show.

HERE'S LOOKING AT YOU, MR. PRESIDENT

Bullsh*t!

Actor and future president of the United States Ronald Reagan nearly played the iconic role of Rick Blaine in *Casablanca*.

Truth:

Once he got into politics, Reagan's movie star status became a bit overstated—he was never more than a second-tier star of B-movies like the chimp comedy *Bedtime for Bonzo* and the war movie *Hellcats of the Navy*. One little bit of fake news from the early '40s helped perpetuate the myth that Reagan had been a screen legend. In 1942, Warner Bros. planted a news release with *The Hollywood Reporter* announcing that Reagan would be starring in *Casablanca*—it was a ploy to keep Reagan in the gossip columns. But he never got the part, nor was he even considered for such a major movie.

CRACKING UP

Bullsh*t!

Humpty Dumpty is an egg.

Truth:

Nowhere in the original, four-line poem does it say that the figure who fell off a wall and couldn't be reassembled by all the king's horses and all the king's men is an egg. That idea entered the collective mind when Lewis Carroll depicted Humpty Dumpty as an egg in his extremely popular 1871 book *Through the Looking-Glass*.

A TRUE DISCOVERY

Bullsh*t!

Located on the Sunset Strip in Hollywood, Schwab's was a soda fountain, restaurant, and movie industry hangout. One day in 1937, teenager Judy Turner skipped a class to grab a Coke at Schwab's, and movie director Mervyn Le Roy was so entranced by her beauty, he offered her a screen test, and she was soon on her way to stardom as "Lana" Turner.

Truth:

Turner was discovered at a different hangout called the Top Hat, and it was *The Hollywood Reporter* publisher Billy Wilkerson who spotted her, not Le Roy. When Turner became a star, the Top Hat commemorated her discovery with a plaque. The story was good for business, and so when the Top Hat closed, Schwab's stole the story and claimed that it had happened there.

SYNCHRONIZE!

Bullsh*t!

Pink Floyd made its 1973 album *Dark Side of the Moon* to sync up with the 1939 classic movie *The Wizard of Oz*.

Truth:

Who knows how many listening/viewing parties this rumor inspired when it first spread in the late '90s? Admittedly, there are some ways the lyrics on the record line up with the images on the screen—"Brain Damage" starts when the Scarecrow starts singing "If I Only Had a Brain," and "The Great Gig in the Sky" plays during the tornado sequence. But it's all just a weird coincidence. MTV asked *Dark Side* engineer Alan Parsons about it, and he said "there simply wasn't the mechanics" to play videotapes in the recording studio...especially since VHS cassettes didn't exist in the early 1970s.

WARDROBE MALFUNCTION

Bullsh*t!

The 2004 Super Bowl Halftime Show was tainted by "Nipplegate": Justin Timberlake ripped off a piece of Janet Jackson's clothing, accidentally exposing her nipple to the world.

Truth:

It was seemingly planned. Timberlake sang the lyric "gonna have you naked by the end of the song" right before he tore away Jackson's breastplate. While most of Jackson's breast was visible, the most offensive-to-censors part, the nipple, was covered by a pasty (which also suggests the whole bit was premeditated).

DEAN'S DEATH DEBUNKED

Bullsh*t!

James Dean died at age 24 in 1955 after he crashed his Porsche Spyder into another car at about 90 miles per hour.

Truth:

That is how he died, but the *Rebel Without a Cause* star wasn't driving as recklessly as presumed. A 2005 inquest revealed that Dean was only going about 70 miles per hour, and had braked hard—not sped up—to avoid that other vehicle.

IT WENT WITH THE WIND

Bullsh*t!

Vivien Leigh won a talent search to land the role of Scarlett O'Hara in *Gone With the Wind*.

Truth:

The movie was heavily anticipated and in production for three years before its release in 1939, and producer David O. Selznick publicly struggled to find the perfect actress to play O'Hara, landing on Vivien Leigh after interviewing and auditioning 1,400 women. But that was all a publicity stunt. He may have reviewed that many candidates, but he actively pursued Leigh for more than a year before she agreed to take the part.

The War of the Worlds "Hysteria" of 1938

In a classic example of "mass hysteria," thousands of New Jersey residents fled their homes on October 30, 1938, and ran for the hills in terror when they believed that an alien invasion was underway. UFOs hadn't really landed in the Garden State, of course. These poor fools had been duped by a radio show. For the CBS radio anthology *The Mercury Theatre on the Air*, Orson Wells directed and narrated an innovative adaptation of H.G. Wells' 1898 alien invasion novel *The War of the Worlds*, presented as a mock, as-it-happens, breaking news broadcast.

But did countless people really freak out? No, they most certainly did not. The C.E. Hooper company phoned 5,000 homes to conduct its night radio ratings survey. Only 2 percent said they checked out *The Mercury Theatre*, and a few cities (including Boston) didn't even air the show that night, because it wasn't a terribly popular show. The notion that some radio show caused a mass panic was falsely reported by major newspapers of the day. The reason: Radio, and radio-delivered news especially, was a threat to business. They wanted to discredit the medium as irresponsible and dangerous...so that people would keep buying newspapers.

VIDEO TENNIS, ANYONE?

Bullsh*t!

Pong was the first video game.

Truth:

While *Pong* was the first popular video game, hitting arcades in 1972, it wasn't the first game, or even the first tennis-simulating video game. Back in 1958, computer think-tank Brookhaven National Laboratory in New York created *Tennis for Two* to show off what its machines could do.

MOVIE MAGIC

Bullsh*t!

"Lights, camera, action" is what directors say on film sets when it's time to shoot a scene.

Truth:

This comes from old movies about making movies, and it's an over-simplification of the complicated process of setting up a shot. Lights take a long time to get right, and they're ready to go by the time a director calls "action" as a prompt to the actors. (They never say "camera," though.)

WE READ IT IN A MAGAZINE

Bullsh*t!

Elton John's 1973 hit "Bennie and the Jets" is a live recording taken from a concert.

Truth:

It's a song about rock stars and rock concerts, but John and his band recorded it in a studio and added applause and audience noise tracks to create the feeling of a live show.

HEY HEY, WE'RE THE MANSONS

Bullsh*t!

Before his notorious murder spree, Charles Manson auditioned for the Monkees.

Truth:

Manson was a failed rock musician and even convinced the Beach Boys to record one of his songs, but when the open call for the Monkees went out in 1965, Manson was in jail on a forgery charge.

Chapter 10

I Heard it Somewhere

Sorry, but your mother and most movies totally lied to you about pretty much everything.

If a criminal confronts someone he suspects of being an undercover police officer, the incognito cop must come clean and admit it when asked. Otherwise, any crimes the criminal commits can be legally dismissed as "entrapment."

Truth:

That's just on cop shows. Undercover cops can and do lie about their identities to protect themselves and their cases.

DOWN TO THE WIRE

*Bullsh*t!*

Defusing a bomb is as easy as cutting the correct wire.

Truth:

It's not like in the movies. A bomb is usually a sophisticated bit of scientific weaponry. There's a lot more to it than just looking for the right color of wire to cut (if the wires are even colored).

NOT SO LOUD

*Bullsh*t!*

Silencers silence the sound of a fired gun.

Truth:

The gun industry prefers to call silencers the more accurate "suppressors."

RIGHT TURN

Bullsh*t!

If police arrest a suspect and don't read them their Miranda rights, that's a technicality that can get the case overturned.

Truth:

Police have to give the Miranda warning only to suspects they're taking into custody and then plan to interrogate. If they ask a bunch of questions without reading the suspect their rights, anything the suspect says cannot be used in court.

TERRITORIAL DISPUTE

Bullsh*t!

Police officers cannot operate outside their jurisdiction.

Truth:

A court can grant exceptions, while many states freely allow police to work outside of their area—city cops may have the right to conduct law enforcement activities in a surrounding county, for example.

THERE YOU ARE

Bullsh*t!

A caller has to be kept on the line for at least 60 seconds in order to trace the call.

Truth:

This dramatic moment only happens in the movies. Authorities can trace a phone call as soon as it's been placed.

PHONING IT IN

Bullsh*t!
Police let an arrested person make one phone call.

Truth:
This is the law in a handful of states. Elsewhere, it's merely a courtesy that police may or may not extend.

'TIL DEATH DO YOU PART

Bullsh*t!
Half of all marriages end in divorce.

Truth:
Love wins! That stat was taken from state of Nevada records, where getting a divorce is relatively fast and easy. In other states, people make it work. Statistics indicate that 70 to 75 percent of people who got married in the 1990s are *still* married to the same people.

POLICING THE WORLD

Bullsh*t!
Interpol is a worldwide police agency.

Truth:
It's an organization that allows law enforcement around the world to communicate and work together, but it's not a standalone police force.

ADVANCED DEGREE

Bullsh*t!
Every human is connected to every other human via six degrees of separation.

Truth:
That's the result of a 1967 study, but more recent ones find that the average rate of separation is nine.

SCHOOL DAYS

Bullsh*t!
Your permanent record will follow you around forever, and negative entries will affect your ability to find employment.

Truth:
It's permanent in that it lasts until you graduate high school. Even then, your disciplinary and attendance records can't be shared with anyone except you.

YOU'VE GOT MAIL

Bullsh*t!
Mailing a document to yourself is a minor but valid form of copyright protection.

Truth:
This doesn't provide any legal protection for work in the United States.

A STINK ABOUT INK

Bullsh*t!
If you're Jewish and get a tattoo, you can't be buried in a Jewish cemetery.

Truth:
The Torah's Book of Leviticus forbids tattoos, but Judaism itself doesn't shut out adherents who got inked.

JUST A MAN

Bullsh*t!
The Buddha is the overarching deity of Buddhism.

Truth:
Various sects consider the Buddha to be a wise man or savior, but he's not viewed as an omnipotent, supernatural being.

CONCEIVING CONCEPTION

Bullsh*t!
Immaculate Conception refers to the article of Christian faith that Jesus Christ was born to a virgin mother.

Truth:
It refers to a bit of Catholic dogma—that Jesus's mother, Mary, was without the taint of original sin from the moment of *her* conception.

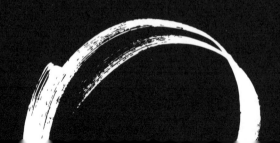

RIGHT AWAY

Bullsh*t!
The pope is infallible, and therefore always right.

Truth:
Only in statements judged to be of divine proclamation.

JUST THE TICKET

Bullsh*t!
Red cars get more speeding tickets than cars in any other shade.

Truth:
Because sports cars are often red—and are made to be driven fast—there's a misconception that *all* red cars get more than their fair share of tickets. They don't.

HEAVENLY

Bullsh*t!
The Koran guarantees that 72 virgins in heaven await religious martyrs.

Truth:
The holy text of Islam promises *houris*, or companions, to everyone who makes it to heaven, but no specific number is given.

GET IT IN WRITING

Bullsh*t!

A *fatwa* is a death sentence handed down from a high-ranking Islamic official.

Truth:

It's a written opinion of a legal matter of any kind handed down by an Islamic scholar, and it's not legally binding.

FREAKS COME OUT AT NIGHT

Bullsh*t!

The average person swallows eight to 10 spiders a year while they're sleeping.

Truth:

It's an urban legend. A sleeping body sends off several warning signs to the average skittish spider, such as snoring and a chest that heaves up and down with every breath.

IT CAN'T WAIT

Bullsh*t!

You have to wait for a person to be gone for 24 hours before you file a missing persons report.

Truth:

Not at all. In the event of an unexpected or sudden absence, police need to know right away.

GOING DEEP

Bullsh*t!
The "Deep Web" is a lawless part of the Internet where criminals buy and sell drugs, bank account numbers, and pornography.

Truth:
You can find all that stuff on the "Dark Web," a tiny portion of the Deep Web. The Deep Web is just anything that search engines don't index and thus make accessible—private stuff like databases and research libraries.

HIDING IN PLAIN SIGHT

Bullsh*t!
Browsing the Internet in "private" or "incognito" mode leaves no trace of your activities.

Truth:
Websites you visit in private mode may not show up in your browser history, but there's still a record of them with your Internet service provider.

SKETCHING IT OUT

Bullsh*t!
Spam—unwanted, unsolicited email—is named after Spam, the polarizing canned meat product.

Truth:
Early Internet users named it after the 1970 *Monty Python's Flying Circus* sketch set in a diner where every item on the menu has some form of Spam in it.

GETTING THINGS ONLINE

Bullsh*t!
The "World Wide Web" and "the Internet" are the same thing.

Truth:
The World Wide Web is a way to navigate the Internet. It's a user-friendly tool to pore through all the information shared by computers.

THE CHOICE IS YOURS

Bullsh*t!
If convicted of certain crimes, individuals can choose military service instead of prison.

Truth:
No branch of the U.S. Armed Forces has allowed this since at least the 1980s.

SHOW THEM THE DOOR

Bullsh*t!
The safest place to wait out an earthquake is in a doorway.

Truth:
A widely distributed photograph of an earthquake in California decades ago pictured a person standing in a doorway, the only part of their adobe-style home left standing. But that's because doorways in that style of house—and more or less *only* that style of house—are reinforced. In the average home, standing in a doorway isn't safe at all, leaving you a target for falling or flying objects.

OFF THE DEEP END

Bullsh*t!

Municipal swimming pools employ a chemical that makes urine instantly visible.

Truth:

That's just something parents tell their kids so they won't pee in the pool.

REAL LIFE ISN'T *DIE HARD*

Bullsh*t!

A building's air ducts can be used as escape tunnels.

Truth:

Air ducts are too small for adults to climb through.

MAINTENANCE REQUIRED

Bullsh*t!

You should change your car's oil every 3,000 miles to ensure everything runs properly.

Truth:

So say automotive service companies. Car manufacturers say it's safe to go as many as 7,500 miles between oil changes.

AW, SHOOT

Bullsh*t!

Getting shot can send a person flying across the room.

Truth:

A bullet is small, and a fired one doesn't pack the force or velocity to propel a human being into the air.

FEELING WOOZY

Bullsh*t!

Breathing chloroform will instantly cause a person to pass out.

Truth:

It takes five minutes of constant inhalation for chloroform to put somebody to sleep.

JUST SIGN HERE, DEAR

Bullsh*t!

A religious marriage ceremony is legally binding.

Truth:

Nope. That's why the bride and groom have to sign so many forms on their big day—those are for the government.

SNOT TRUE

Bullsh*t!

We say "God bless you" when others sneeze because it's an old custom from the days when people thought sneezing involved your soul trying to escape.

Truth:

In the 6th century, a plague hit Europe, and Pope Gregory instructed Christians to say "God bless you" when someone sneezed, a mini-prayer asking the heavens above to spare this poor, plague-stricken person.

HOW SWEET IT IS

Bullsh*t!

Pouring sugar in a car's gas tank is a nasty prank that can destroy the engine.

Truth:

Sugar doesn't dissolve in gasoline, which means it doesn't turn into engine-clogging sludge.

RIGHT PLACE, RIGHT TINE

Bullsh*t!

To be a proper, safe driver, keep your hands on the steering wheel at the "10 and 2" positions.

Truth:

Before the advent of power steering, placing the hands just above the middle of the wheel gave the driver the extra "oomph" and leverage it needed to turn well. Experts say "9 and 3" are the new "10 and 2."

JUST A THOUGHT

Bullsh*t!

Men think about sex every seven seconds.

Truth:

This is a facetious exaggeration gently mocking men's lusty ways. According to the groundbreaking Kinsey Report on human sexuality, about half of men think about sex "several" times a day...not every seven seconds.

DRAINING

Bullsh*t!

You have to let a battery (in a phone, or laptop computer, for example) completely drain before charging it again, or this will lead to diminished battery life over time.

Truth:

That's not how rechargeable lithium-ion batteries work. No matter where the percentage bar is at when you plug it in, the battery won't weaken.

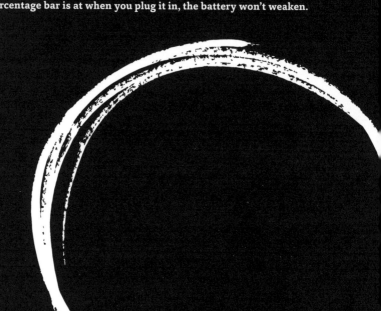

Chapter 11

I Never Said That!

Some familiar quotes...that weren't quite said the way that everybody thinks they were said.

YEAR IT IS

Bullsh*t!

"And in the end, it's not the years in your life that count. It's the life in your years."

Truth:

A wise aphorism from good ol' "Honest Abe" himself, Abraham Lincoln? It really stems from an advertisement. In 1947, Dr. Edward J. Stieglitz published a book about aging called *The Second Forty Years*. Print ads included that statement as the tagline.

SHINE ON

Bullsh*t!

"All that glitters is not gold."

Truth:

A proverb that means "buyer beware" or "things may not be what they seem," it's a misquote of a Shakespeare line. In *The Merchant of Venice*, the Prince of Morocco advises, "All that glisters is not gold." Glisters is a now-obscure word that means...glitters.

CLOSE, BUT NO VOLTAIRE

Bullsh*t!

"I disapprove of what you say, but I will defend to the death your right to say it."

Truth:

French literary icon Voltaire didn't originate this utterance about the importance of free speech. In the early 1900s, Evelyn Beatrice Hall wrote two books about Voltaire—*The Life of Voltaire* and *The Friends of Voltaire*. It's in the latter where she originated the quote.

TIME TO REFLECT

Bullsh*t!

"Mirror, mirror, on the wall, who's the fairest of them all?"

Truth:

The Evil Queen in *Snow White and the Seven Dwarfs* implores "Magic Mirror on the wall, who is the fairest one of all?"

WHO'S IN CHARGE?

Bullsh*t!

"To learn who rules over you, simply find out whom you are not allowed to criticize."

Truth:

Here's another seemingly cleverly worded bit of wit and wisdom from Voltaire, often used to garner anti-authoritarian sentiment. Its origin is dark and ugly. Kevin Strom, a Neo-Nazi writer, coined the phrase in the late 20th century, and the people he claims he was "not allowed to criticize" are the Jewish people he was convinced secretly ran the world.

CLOTHES MAKE THE WOMAN

Bullsh*t!

"Your clothes should be tight enough to show you're a woman but loose enough to show you're a lady."

Truth:

Not a flirty and suggestive Marilyn Monroe quote. It was uttered by the witty, Oscar-winning costume designer (and basis for *The Incredibles'* Edna Mode) Edith Head.

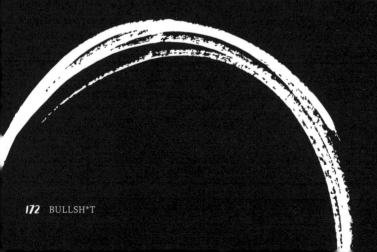

THIS ONE IS A WINNER

Bullsh*t!

"Winning isn't everything. It's the only thing."

Truth:

It's attributed to legendary football coach Vince Lombardi—some tough words to motivate his Green Bay Packers squads. Lombardi claimed to have never said it, although he was known to offer up a variant: "Winning isn't a sometime thing; it's an all the time thing." He was riffing on the actual quote, which originated with UCLA football coach Red Sanders.

BUT NOT ANYMORE!

Bullsh*t!

"There's a sucker born every minute."

Truth:

Circus exhibitor and promoter P.T. Barnum supposedly said this, but it was actually said by rival David Hannum. Barnum had created a copy of one of Hannum's exhibitions and successfully passed it off as the original, prompting Hannum to say what he said.

FOOLS!

Bullsh*t!

"You can fool all the people some of the time and some of the people all the time, but you cannot fool all the people all the time."

Truth:

This quote appeared anonymously in the 1880s, spread, and before long was attributed to the beloved and wise Abraham Lincoln. It didn't spontaneously appear, however. It's based on a French aphorism that dates to the 1684 book *Traité de la Vérité de la Religion Chrétienne* by French writer Jacques Abbadie. The line translates to English as "One can fool some men, or fool all men in some places and times, but one cannot fool all men in all places and ages."

HEARTS AND MINDS

Bullsh*t!

"If you're not liberal when you're 25, you have no heart. If you're not a conservative by the time you're 35, you have no brain."

Truth:

This succinct summarization of how one's politics change with age is offered up as an example of the great wisdom of Winston Churchill. The British prime minister got more liberal the older he got, so it wouldn't make sense if he'd said it. He didn't—it's derived from a quote in an 1875 book by French writer Jules Claretie.

TAKE A WALK

Bullsh*t!
"If you're going through hell, keep going."

Truth:
A circa-World War II quote from Winston Churchill? Nope. It's from a story in a 1943 issue of the *Christian Science Sentinel* by editor John Randall Dunn, who presented it as an age-old proverb. "Someone once asked a man how he was. He replied, 'I'm going through hell!' Said his friend: 'Well, keep on going. That is no place to stop!'"

READY, AIM...

Bullsh*t!
"Don't fire 'til you see the whites of their eyes!"

Truth:
Right quote, but wrong war (and so the wrong guy). Many history books claim that General Andrew Jackson said this to his troops at the dawn of the Battle of New Orleans regarding British troops in the War of 1812. Who really said it: Colonel William Prescott of the Continental Army at the Battle of Bunker Bill in 1775, during the American Revolution.

SMOKE 'EM IF YOU GOT 'EM

Bullsh*t!

"Sometimes a cigar is just a cigar."

Truth:

It's one of the most famous quotes attributed to Sigmund Freud, the eminently quotable "father of psychoanalysis," a field in which doctors find the true meaning behind their patients' thoughts, actions, and, in the case of Freud, their dreams. But hey, this quote suggests, not *everything* has meaning. Freud never said it. *The Jungle Book* author Rudyard Kipling did... kind of. In his poem "The Betrothed," he wrote, "A woman is only a woman, but a good cigar is a smoke." (Whatever *that* means.)

LOVE AND MARRIAGE

Bullsh*t!

Socialite Lady Astor and Winston Churchill ran in the same circles, but didn't care for each other. At a fancy dinner one night, Astor told Churchill, "If I were married to you, I'd put poison in your coffee." Churchill's witty retort: "If I were married to you, I'd drink it."

Truth:

Such an exchange actually did take place, although it was between Lady Astor and English politician Lord Birkinhead...who was repeating a very old joke.

LIES BY HORSEBACK

Bullsh*t!

"The British are coming!"

Truth:

If Paul Revere were supposed to secretly inform Revolutionary operatives about incoming British soldiers, why would he ride through a town shouting those exact words? He—and his freedom-fighting cohorts—would've been immediately arrested by crown loyalists and British army patrol officers. Revere actually shouted the coded message, "The rears are coming out." (He also didn't go it alone—another freedom fighter named Sybil Ludington got the word out too. Some historians say she probably informed way more people than did Revere.)

THE TRUTH ABOUT LYING

Bullsh*t!

"A lie can travel halfway around the world while the truth is putting on its shoes."

Truth:

This quip about the viral nature of misinformation has been most commonly attributed to quote machines like Mark Twain, Winston Churchill, Thomas Jefferson, and, oddly enough, Ann Landers. But it's really a reworking of something said by 18th-century satirist and *Gulliver's Travels* author Jonathan Swift: "Falsehood flies, and truth comes limping after it."

IT'S A MYSTERY

Bullsh*t!

"Elementary, my dear Watson!"

Truth:

It's the definitive Sherlock Holmes quote and self-proclamation of genius, but Sir Arthur Conan Doyle's fictional detective never said that in 56 short stories and four novels. In *The Adventure of the Crooked Man*, Holmes says, "I have the advantage of knowing your habits, my dear Watson," and after a few lines of dialogue between himself and Watson, he interjects, "Elementary."

THE DARTH TRUTH

Bullsh*t!

"Luke, I am your father!"

Truth:

Perhaps the most famous movie "spoiler" of all time, this one condensed over time from a couple lines of dialogue into a snappy catchphrase. Darth Vader from *The Empire Strikes Back* would *never* be so informal as to call someone by their first name. The scene plays out like this:

DARTH VADER: Obi Wan never told you what happened to your father.
LUKE: He told me enough. He told me *you* killed him.
DARTH VADER: No, *I* am your father!

YOU BETCHA, RUSSIA!

Bullsh*t!
"I can see Russia from my house."

Truth:
One of the breakout personalities of the 2008 election was Republican vice presidential candidate Sarah Palin, Alaska governor and little known outside of her state before she was thrust into the spotlight. Prone to folksy sayings, she didn't say this one—it's a line from a *Saturday Night Live* sketch in which Tina Fey parodied Palin. What Palin actually said, that Fey referenced: "In the middle of the Bering Strait are two small, sparsely populated islands: Big Diomede, which sits in Russian territory, and Little Diomede, which is part of the United States. At their closest, these two islands are a little less than two and a half miles apart, which means that, on a clear day, you can definitely see one from the other."

AN INSANE STORY

Bullsh*t!
"Insanity is doing the same thing over and over again and expecting different results."

Truth:
Albert Einstein didn't say it. The quote dates back only to 1981 and the addiction recovery realm. In a newspaper article about Al-Anon, an organization that helps the families of alcoholics, the author mentions that one of the group's steps is to "restore [its members] to sanity." One woman told the reporter, "Insanity is doing the same thing over and over again and expecting different results." As such organizations treasure and protect anonymity, the identity of its speaker was never divulged.

LADIES AND GENTLEMEN

Bullsh*t!

"Women who seek to be equal with men lack ambition."

Truth:

An empowering statement of active feminism, sure, but it wasn't coined by Marilyn Monroe, or any other woman for that matter. LSD advocate and 1960s thought leader Timothy Leary said it.

ANONYMOUS WOMEN OFTEN MAKE HISTORY

Bullsh*t!

"Well-behaved women seldom make history."

Truth:

Sometimes attributed to Marilyn Monroe, or often left unattributed on millions of T-shirts, bumper stickers, and coffee mugs as if it were a timeless proverb, it was coined by college professor Laurel Thatcher Ulrich in an article in an academic journal in 1976.

LET'S PLAY

Bullsh*t!
"Play it again, Sam."

Truth:
Humphrey Bogart doesn't say that line In *Casablanca*. Nobody does. This is the exchange:
ILSA (Ingrid Bergman): Play it once, Sam. For old times' sake.
SAM (Dooley Wilson): I don't know what you mean, Miss Ilsa.
ILSA: Play it, Sam. Play "As Time Goes By."

A FACT ABOUT FACTS

Bullsh*t!
"Just the facts, ma'am."

Truth:
It sounds like a thing that stoic, no-nonsense, by-the-book cop Joe Friday (Jack Webb) would've said to a witness on the classic TV show *Dragnet*. He did once say, "All we want are the facts, ma'am," but "Just the facts, ma'am" comes from "St. George and the Dragonet," a *Dragnet*-mocking novelty record by Stan Freberg that hit #1 in 1953.

WHERE NO LIE
HAS GONE BEFORE

Bullsh*t!

"Beam me up, Scotty!"

Truth:

This "iconic" line of Captain Kirk's from *Star Trek* was never stated in this, its most quoted variant. Kirk rarely visited hostile alien planets alone, so he usually said something like "Beam us up," while in *Star Trek IV: The Voyage Home*, he says, "Scotty, beam me up."

IT CAME FROM OUTER SPACE

Bullsh*t!

"The needs of the many outweigh the needs of the few."

Truth:

It sounds like it's a piece of ancient wisdom from a philosopher, politician, or religious figure. It originated in the 1982 movie *Star Trek II: The Wrath of Khan*. Spock said it.

STICK AROUND

Bullsh*t!

"Speak softly and carry a big stick."

Truth:

Theodore Roosevelt supposedly said it, expressing his approach to diplomacy and defense. While he popularized it in the West, the actual quote involved Roosevelt quoting the source: "I have always been fond of the West African proverb, 'Speak softly and carry a big stick, you will go far.'"

THE LUCKY ONE

Bullsh*t!

"Do you feel lucky, punk?"

Truth:

In the 1971 movie *Dirty Harry*, grizzled cop Harry Callahan (Clint Eastwood) delivers a much longer line to a criminal he's threatening with a gun: "You've got ask yourself one question. Do I feel lucky? Well, do ya, punk?"

"Let them eat cake!"

Its often cited as proof that French ruler Marie Antoinette was so out of touch that she had no idea how or why the people of France were starving...and that the quote got out and enraged the people so much that it kicked the French Revolution into high gear. (Long story short: Marie Antoinette would soon be separated from her head.) This quote had nothing to do with any of that. In his 1767 book *Confessions*, French writer Jean-Jacques Rousseau spoke of a "princess" who responded to news of peasants with no food with the suggestion, "If they have no bread, let them eat cake!" He was likely referring to Maria Theresa of Spain...because in 1767 Marie Antoinette wasn't even in power yet.

Chapter 12

A Holiday Away From the Truth

Celebrate and get festive by pulling the
party hat up off of your eyes and ears for
these true stories behind holidays and
holiday-adjacent figures.

WHERE ARE WE?

Bullsh*t!

Columbus Day commemorates the day that Christopher Columbus landed his ships on mainland North America in October 1492.

Truth:

Columbus and company found landfall on some of the many islands that lay off the southeastern coast of North America, notably Hispaniola, which is now home to Haiti and the Dominican Republic.

BORN ON THE 2ND OF JULY

Bullsh*t!

The United States of America was born on July 4, 1776, when the Second Continental Congress signed the Declaration of Independence.

Truth:

The representative body voted in the affirmative for independence on July 2, and the document was approved and printed on July 4. It got all the signatures it needed on August 2.

IRISH YOU KNEW

Bullsh*t!

St. Patrick, the patron saint of Ireland and namesake of St. Patrick's Day, was Irish.

Truth:

His real name is Palladius and he was born in Scotland in the 4th century. As a teenager, he was kidnapped and sold into slavery in Ireland, but later escaped, returned to Scotland, joined a monastery, and then became a missionary in Ireland.

FOOLISH

Bullsh*t!

April Fool's Day began when Europe switched to a new calendar, and those who still followed the old one—which celebrated the new year on April 1— were considered fools worthy of derision and pranks.

Truth:

There's absolutely no evidence that this is true. For one, different countries adopted the Gregorian calendar (with its start on January 1) at different times, sometimes decades apart.

HAPPY CHRISTMAS

Bullsh*t!

Suicide rates skyrocket during Christmastime—people already depressed just can't bear all that forced comfort and joy.

Truth:

Suicide rates hit their lowest point in the U.S. in December, on average, but surge in the fall and spring.

WE [ ] KINGS

Bullsh*t!

Baby Jesus was visited in his manger by three kings.

Truth:

The Bible doesn't specify the specific number of "magi" that visited Jesus, nor that they were kings. It's an artistic tradition dating back to the 3rd century to depict three kings in nativity scenes…and they weren't even there. According to the Bible, the magi (however many there were) paid their visit months later.

FIRST WE FEAST

Bullsh*t!

The Pilgrims and local Native Americans held the first Thanksgiving in Plymouth colony in 1621.

Truth:

Thanksgiving is a centuries-old tradition in England, but it's more of a harvest festival, with feasts, yes, but also dancing and games. The staid and somber Pilgrims eliminated all of that (except for the feasting) for their first Thanksgiving in the New World, turning it into a reflective, religious occasion.

HAPPY PHEASANT DAY!

Bullsh*t!

The Pilgrims served turkey at the first American Thanksgiving.

Truth:

Contemporary accounts note that the Pilgrims and their guests dined on venison, pheasant, goose, and duck.

HAPPY DEATH-DAY

Bullsh*t!

St. Patrick's Day marks St. Patrick's birthday.

Truth:

A Catholic saint's feast day commemorates the day of their death, not the day of their birth.

NAP TIME

Bullsh*t!

Everybody gets sleepy on Thanksgiving because of tryptophan, a naturally occurring sedative found in turkey.

Truth:

There's a very small amount of tryptophan in turkey. People need a long post-dinner / pre-pie nap on Turkey Day because they just ate a gigantic, carbohydrate-laden meal.

THE DAY AFTER

Bullsh*t!

Black Friday is so named because the high level of consumer spending puts so many retail companies into the profit zone for the year, or "in the black."

Truth:

It was coined to describe a catastrophic, widespread work shortage. In the 1950s, massive numbers of American started calling in sick to work on the Friday after Thanksgiving, so as to give themselves a four-day weekend.

MERRY CHRISTMAS

Bullsh*t!

Jesus Christ was born on December 25.

Truth:

There's nothing in the Bible that suggests that date. An observance of Christ's birthday was chosen to correspond with (and overcome) pagan winter festivals. Bible scholars think that Jesus was most likely born in September or October.

LEAF IT ALONE

Bullsh*t!

Poinsettias, while a lovely and traditional part of Christmas, are poisonous to humans and cats.

Truth:

You shouldn't start making a salad or anything, but they're only mildly irritating to the digestive systems of both humans and felines.

WHAT A SAINT

Bullsh*t!

Valentine's Day originates with Valentine, a 3rd-century Catholic priest who defied Roman authorities and performed marriages for loving couples, and was put to death for it.

Truth:

There are numerous St. Valentines from the 3rd century, and of the two who share the Feast of St. Valentine on February 14, little is known about them. The story that one of them performed marriages is a romantic notion invented centuries later by a martyr-worshipping cult.

SHOP 'TIL YOU DROP

Bullsh*t!

In terms of revenue and volume, Black Friday is the biggest shopping day of the year.

Truth:

While Black Friday kicks off the Christmas shopping season, a lot of people buy gifts at the last minute. The busiest day of the year in stores is generally December 23, and/or the last Saturday before Christmas.

BARNSTORMING

Bullsh*t!
Jesus was born in a barn.

Truth:
Because a manger (a horse-feeding trough) served as a makeshift bassinet for the baby Jesus, the notion that he was born in a barn, a place where one would be most likely to find a manger, persisted. It's more likely that Jesus was born in a cave, or in a private home (his mother's husband, Joseph, was from Bethlehem and knew people there), but in a common living area as opposed to a bedroom.

HE'S CRAFTY

Bullsh*t!
Jesus Christ was a carpenter.

Truth:
The Gospels of the Bible, which tell the story of Jesus, were written in Greek. Translations misread the Greek word for "home builder" as carpenter, but since in Judea buildings were by and large constructed out of stone, Jesus was more than likely a stone mason.

SNAKED

Bullsh*t!
St. Patrick drove the snakes out of Ireland.

Truth:
There weren't any snakes in Ireland at that time. The tales that he did that are metaphorical—the snakes are pagan religions he excised by spreading Christianity.

X MARKS THE SPOT

Bullsh*t!

"Xmas" is a secularization of the word Christmas, separating the holiday from its religious origins.

Truth:

The "X" stands for Christ. It's been used as an abbreviation by religious scholars since the 11th century.

A THANKSGIVING CAROL

Bullsh*t!

The universally known "Jingle Bells" is a Christmas carol.

Truth:

Like "Over the River and Through the Woods," it depicts a long journey…to Thanksgiving dinner. It was first performed to celebrate *that* holiday in 1857.

NOT QUITE RIGHT

Bullsh*t!
Cinco de Mayo is Mexico's Independence Day.

Truth:
The May 5th holiday recognizes the victory of the Mexican army over the French in the 1862 Battle of Puebla, part of the Franco-Mexican War. It's not even that big of a holiday in Mexico.

OLD GLORY

Bullsh*t!
Betsy Ross designed the American flag.

Truth:
Several different flags were used in colonial times, but most used the "Union Jack" symbol of England in some way. Owing to the need for a new cultural identity and to avoid confusion on the American Revolution battlefield, the Continental Congress passed a bill in June 1777 calling for a flag consisting of 13 red and white alternating stripes and 13 white stars on a blue field. New Jersey representative (and designer) Francis Hopkinson chose those elements and sent them along to someone else to execute. Folklore says Betsy Ross did that, but there's no evidence that she actually did.

Trick-or-Treaters Beware!

Parents, check your kids' Halloween candy— somebody could have poisoned it, or hidden a dangerous razor blade inside a piece, right? Actually, there are no accounts of kids in America dying from eating Halloween candy tampered with by strangers. This annual mass hysteria likely stems from a 1974 case in which a boy from Texas died after eating Pixy Stix laced with cyanide; police discovered the murder weapon had been snuck into the boy's candy stash by his own father. There have been other cases of children who died right after Halloween, and while poisoned candy was suspected, that cause was ruled out by toxicology tests every time.

Chapter 13

No, Really, It's True

Now let's switch things up. These facts are so preposterous that they just have to be made up. But, amazingly, they're 100 percent true.

OLD SCHOOL

Bullsh*t!

Oxford University in England is older than the Aztec civilization of the Americas?

Truth:

Oxford opened its doors in 1096, while the Aztecs really got going with the founding of the city of Tenochtitlan in 1325.

TIME FLIES

Bullsh*t!

A day on Venus lasts longer than a year on Venus?

Truth:

In this solar system, a "day" is the amount of time it takes a planet to rotate on its axis, while a "year" is the period of a planet's "revolution," or a full orbit around the sun. On Earth, a day consists of 24 hours, and a revolution takes 365 days. It takes Venus 243 Earth days to spin on its axis (a day), but just 225 Earth days to revolve around the sun (a year).

JUST LIKE PARADISE

Bullsh*t!

People used to rent pineapples to look rich?

Truth:

In the 1700s and 1800s, it took a lot of time and money to import pineapples from distant, tropical lands. Having one was a sign of wealth, as they cost about $8,000 in today's dollars. Rich people would display their fancy pineapple during parties, while slightly less wealthy people in the U.S. and England simply rented one.

HIDE YOUR TOOTHBRUSH

Bullsh*t!
A fine mist of bacteria-laden spray spreads throughout the bathroom after you flush the toilet?

Truth:
This is called "toilet plume." The sheer force of the flush sends a spray of microscopic particles of whatever was in the commode into the air. Those bits come to rest as far as six feet away from the toilet.

IT TAKES A LICKING

Bullsh*t!
It takes about 300 licks to get to the center of a Tootsie Pop?

Truth:
It's the basis of a famous and long-running ad campaign for the sucker-with-a-heart-of-chocolate: "How many licks does it take to get to the center of a Tootsie Pop?" A study at Purdue University used a specially made "licking machine" (which mimicked the tongue) and found that it took an average of 364 licks to get to the middle. Twenty student volunteers needed, on average, 252 licks.

COWBOY UP

Bullsh*t!
There are only two escalators in the entire state of Wyoming?

Truth:
Wyoming is home to less than 600,000 people, so there aren't that many cities, and not too many big buildings either. Both escalators in the entire state are located in banks in the city of Casper.

F*L*U*S*H

Bullsh*t!

So many people used the bathroom all at the same time, immediately after the 1983 finale of *M*A*S*H*—the most-watched program in American TV history—that it nearly flooded the sewers of New York City?

Truth:

A million New Yorkers held it in until the end of "Goodbye, Farewell, and Amen," and then, when they were done, flushed their toilets virtually all at the same time, sending an unprecedented 6.7 million gallons into the city's sewer system.

ROOM TO GROW

Bullsh*t!

Babies are born without kneecaps?

Truth:

It's just a bunch of loose cartilage in the middle of their cute little baby legs. It hardens into knee bones during toddlerhood.

JUMBO SHRIMP

Bullsh*t!

The mantis shrimp can attack enemies with a force comparable to that of a .22 caliber bullet fired from a gun?

Truth:

The mantis has arms that are, for lack of a better term, spring-loaded. That allows it to propel its fists at a velocity of 75 feet per second. It uses this power to smash through the shells of its prey to get to the tasty fish meat inside.

VIVE LE JERRY LEWIS!

Bullsh*t!

The French really do love Jerry Lewis?

Truth:

As much as France loves high culture, the country also appreciates "low comedy," or comic buffoonery, which dates back to 19th-century French theater. Film writers think Lewis caught on in France because his wacky, over-the-top characters appealed to that sensibility while also satirizing the "ugly American" stereotype. It also helped that in the 1960s, Lewis participated in a three-week festival in France that celebrated his movies.

DOLLY'S BIG SECRET

Bullsh*t!

Dolly Parton is heavily tattooed?

Truth:

The queen of country music experienced widespread keloid scars on her body—raised, purple marks. To cover them up, Parton got a ton of pastel-colored tattoos. (And she almost always appears in public wearing long-sleeved dresses.)

TALL TALE

Bullsh*t!

Kareem Abdul-Jabbar was a staff writer on *Veronica Mars*?

Truth:

The NBA legend is very well-rounded. He's written two mystery novels about Mycroft Holmes (Sherlock's brother) and in 2019, he was part of the team that wrote Hulu's revival of the Kristen Bell detective series.

THE BARD'S LADY

Bullsh*t!
The name Jessica didn't exist until William Shakespeare made it up?

Truth:
Shakespeare invented dozens of words, among them dwindle, critic, and lackluster. His 1605 play *The Merchant of Venice* includes the character Jessica, the first such use of the name.

DISNEYLAND OF NO BEARDS

Bullsh*t!
Disney banned men with facial hair from their amusement parks?

Truth:
In 1957, Disneyland (the only Disney park at the time) banned its male workers from rocking long hair, beards, and mustaches, arguing that it didn't jibe with the company's family-friendly image. Facing staffing shortages in 2000, Disney eased up on the ban. Beards are still banned, but trimmed mustaches are okay now.

IT'S THE PITS

Bullsh*t!
Cherry pits are deadly?

Truth:
Whatever you do, don't swallow broken or crushed cherry pits. That breaks the skin, allowing for the release of the cyanide inside. Two cherry pits contain enough cyanide to kill a person.

RIGHT THERE

Bullsh*t!

Babe Ruth really "called his shot" and hit a home run, like he said he was going to do?

Truth:

On the way to his seventh and final championship, the New York Yankees' Babe Ruth stepped up to the plate in Game 3 of the 1932 World Series and pointed at the outfield bleachers. On the very next pitch, he knocked the ball into those bleachers.

ODIOUS ORIGIN

Bullsh*t!

The Nazis invented Fanta?

Truth:

The U.S. government placed a trade embargo on Nazi Germany, meaning Coca-Cola bottlers there couldn't get the ingredients they needed to make Coke. So, they invented orange-flavored Fanta. After the war, the Coca-Cola corporation took the product worldwide.

HEADS UP

Bullsh*t!

A chicken lived without its head for 18 months?

Truth:

In 1945 a farmer named Lloyd Olson chopped the head off one of his roosters. He didn't quite get it all the way off, however, and the chicken's brain stem remained intact. That kept him alive, as did daily feedings of liquid food dropped directly into his open neck. Under the guide of some handlers, Mike the Headless Chicken toured the world as a must-see novelty.

THEY'RE STILL ON THE NAUGHTY LIST

Bullsh*t!

Philadelphia Eagles fans are so tough and rowdy that they once booed Santa Claus?

Truth:

During halftime of the final game of the 1968 regular season—with the Eagles looking to finish with a dismal 2-12 record—the team held a miniature Christmas pageant, consisting of a bunch of cheerleaders and a man dressed as Santa Claus running onto the field. Eagles fans, exhausted by the season, booed and threw snowballs at ol' Saint Nick.

BABIES HAVING BABIES

Bullsh*t!

Aphids are pregnant when they're born?

Truth:

This tiny bug reproduces asexually, generating multiple small versions of itself inside countless tiny eggs. An aphid can get going on that process while it's still waiting to hatch.

GOING FOR A SPIN

Bullsh*t!
Thomas Jefferson invented the swivel chair?

Truth:
As a Founding Father and chief author of the Declaration of Independence, Jefferson kind of invented America...and spinny office chairs, too. In 1774, he attached an iron spindle and caster to the legs of a chair, added the top part, and sat and spun. But why? Jefferson claimed that absent-mindedly spinning around in a chair helped him think.

A PIECE OF THE PIE

Bullsh*t!
There's more pizza in an 18-inch pie than in two 12-inch pies?

Truth:
Measure it yourself. A round, 18-incher offers 254 square inches of pizza. Two 12-inchers provide only 226 inches altogether.

John Tyler's Grandsons Live!

Virginia politician John Tyler served as President of the United States from 1841 to 1845, and as of 2019, his grandsons are still alive. How is this possible? Well, at age 52, Tyler married 22-year-old Julia Gardiner and they had seven children together, with the youngest, Lyon Tyler, arriving when the former president was 63. Lyon Tyler also married a much younger woman and was in his seventies when he fathered Harrison Tyler and Lyon Gardiner Taylor in the 1920s.